AMERICA
AS STORY

AMERICA AS STORY

Historical Fiction for Secondary Schools

ELIZABETH F. HOWARD

American Library Association

CHICAGO AND LONDON 1988

For L.C.H.

Designed by Charles Bozett

Illustration by Joseph Taylor

Composed in Galliard by RT
Associates

Printed on 50-pound Glatfelter,
a pH-neutral stock, and bound
in 10-point Carolina cover stock
by Thomson-Shore, Inc.

∞

Library of Congress Cataloging-in-Publication Data

Howard, Elizabeth Fitzgerald.
America as story.

Includes index.
1. Historical fiction, American—Bibliography. 2. Young adult fiction, American—Bibliography. 3. United States—History—Juvenile fiction—Bibliography. 4. Bibliography—Best books—Young adult fiction. 5. Bibliography—Best books—Historical fiction. 6. High school libraries—Book lists. 7. Junior high school libraries—Book lists.
I. Title.
Z1232.H68   1988   [PS374.H5]   016.813′081′08   88-3453
ISBN 0-8389-0492-0

CONTENTS

INTRODUCTION   xi

ACKNOWLEDGMENTS   xiii

I.   COLONIAL AMERICA   1

Calico Bush *by* Rachel Field   1
Calico Captive *by* Elizabeth George Speare   2
Constance: A Story of Early Plymouth *by* Patricia Clapp   2
A Country of Strangers *by* Conrad Richter   3
The Forest and the Fort *by* Hervey Allen   4
The Light in the Forest *by* Conrad Richter   5
Lusty Wind for Carolina *by* Inglis Fletcher   6
Mercy Short: A Winter Journal, North Boston, 1692–93
    by Norma Farber   6
Roanoke: A Novel of the Lost Colony *by* Sonia Levitin   7
The Sign of the Beaver *by* Elizabeth George Speare   8
The Stratford Devil *by* Claude Clayton Smith   9
Tituba of Salem Village *by* Ann Petry   10
The Witch of Blackbird Pond *by* Elizabeth George Speare   10
Witches' Children: A Story of Salem *by* Patricia Clapp   11

II.   THE AMERICAN REVOLUTION AND THE NEW NATION   13

April Morning *by* Howard Fast   13
Arundel *by* Kenneth Roberts   14
The Bloody Country *by* James Lincoln Collier and
    Christopher Collier   14
Burr *by* Gore Vidal   15
Drums *by* James Boyd   16
The Fighting Ground *by* Avi   17
Freelon Starbird *by* Richard E. Snow   17
The Hessian *by* Howard Fast   18
I'm Deborah Sampson: A Soldier of the American Revolution
    by Patricia Clapp   19

John Treegate's Musket *by* Leonard Wibberley   20
Johnny Tremain *by* Esther Forbes   21
Jump Ship to Freedom *by* James Lincoln Collier and
    Christopher Collier   21
My Brother Sam Is Dead *by* James Lincoln Collier and
    Christopher Collier   22
Oliver Wiswell *by* Kenneth Roberts   23
Rabble in Arms *by* Kenneth Roberts   24
Ruffles and Drums *by* Betty Cavanna   24
Sarah Bishop *by* Scott O'Dell   25
1787 *by* Joan Anderson   26
Time Enough for Drums *by* Ann Rinaldi   27
The Tree of Liberty *by* Elizabeth Page   28
War Comes to Willie Freeman *by* James Lincoln Collier and
    Christopher Collier   29
Who Is Carrie? *by* James Lincoln Collier and
    Christopher Collier   29
The Winter Hero *by* James Lincoln Collier and
    Christopher Collier   30

III.   THE CIVIL WAR AND RECONSTRUCTION   33

Across Five Aprils *by* Irene Hunt   33
Andersonville *by* MacKinlay Kantor   34
The Autobiography of Miss Jane Pittman *by* Ernest J. Gaines   34
Brady *by* Jean Fritz   35
Bring Home the Ghost *by* K. Follis Cheatham   36
The Chaneysville Incident *by* David Bradley   37
Cowslip *by* Betsy Haynes   38
Elkhorn Tavern *by* Douglas C. Jones   38
Freedom Road *by* Howard Fast   39
A Gathering of Days: A New England Girl's Journal,
    1830–1832 *by* Joan Blos   40
Gone with the Wind *by* Margaret Mitchell   41
Hew against the Grain *by* Betty Sue Cummings   42
High Hearts *by* Rita Mae Brown   42
Jubilee *by* Margaret Walker   43
Rifles for Watie *by* Harold Keith   44
Roots: The Saga of an American Family *by* Alex Haley   45
The Sacred Moon Tree *by* Laura Jan Shore   46
The Slave Dancer *by* Paula Fox   46
The Slopes of War: A Novel of Gettysburg *by* N. A. Perez   47

The Tamarack Tree: A Novel of the Siege of Vicksburg
    by Patricia Clapp   48
Tancy *by* Belinda Hurmence   49
This Strange New Feeling *by* Julius Lester   50
Three Days *by* Paxton Davis   51
Turn Homeward, Hannalee *by* Patricia Beatty   51
The 290 *by* Scott O'Dell   52
Unto This Hour *by* Tom Wicker   53
Which Way Freedom? *by* Joyce Hansen   54
A Woman Called Moses *by* Marcy Heidish   55

IV.   WESTWARD EXPANSION AND THE NATIVE
    AMERICAN RESPONSE   57

Arrest Sitting Bull *by* Douglas C. Jones   57
Beyond the Divide *by* Kathryn Lasky   58
The Big Sky *by* A. B. Guthrie   58
Bold Journey: West with Lewis and Clark *by* Charles Bohner   59
Brothers of the Heart: A Story of the Old Northwest
    1837–1838 *by* Joan Blos   60
The Camp Grant Massacre *by* Elliott Arnold   61
Cimarron *by* Edna Ferber   62
The Court-Martial of George Armstrong Custer
    by Douglas C. Jones   62
Crazy Weather *by* Charles McNichols   63
Creek Mary's Blood *by* Dee Brown   64
Gently Touch the Milkweed *by* Lynn Hall   65
Giants in the Earth: A Saga of the Prairie *by* Ole Rolvaag   65
Hannah Herself *by* Ruth Franchere   66
In the Shadow of the Wind *by* Luke Wallin   67
The Keeping-Room *by* Betty Levin   68
Killdeer Mountain *by* Dee Brown   69
A Lantern in Her Hand *by* Bess S. Aldrich   69
Laughing Boy *by* Oliver LaFarge   70
Little Big Man *by* Thomas Berger   71
The Massacre at Fall Creek *by* Jessamyn West   72
My Antonia *by* Willa Cather   73
The No-Return Trail *by* Sonia Levitin   73
Only Earth and Sky Last Forever *by* Nathaniel Benchley   74
Orphan Train *by* James Magnuson and Dorothea G. Petrie   75
The Ox-Bow Incident *by* Walter van Tilburg Clark   76
Prairie Songs *by* Pam Conrad   77

Season of Yellow Leaf *by* Douglas C. Jones   77
Shane *by* Jack Schaefer   78
Sing Down the Moon *by* Scott O'Dell   79
The Snowbird *by* Patricia Calvert   80
The Sodbuster Venture *by* Charlene Joy Talbot   80
Streams to the River, River to the Sea *by* Scott O'Dell   81
Wait for Me, Watch for Me, Eula Bee *by* Patricia Beatty   82
The Way West *by* A. B. Guthrie   83
Young Pioneers *by* Rose Wilder Lane   84

V.   IMMIGRATION, INDUSTRIALIZATION, URBANIZATION   85

After the Dancing Days *by* Margaret I. Rostkowski   85
April Harvest *by* Lillian Budd   86
Dragonwings *by* Laurence Yep   87
The House of Mirth *by* Edith Wharton   87
The Jungle *by* Upton Sinclair   88
The Late George Apley *by* John P. Marquand   89
The Magnificent Ambersons *by* Booth Tarkington   90
Main Street *by* Sinclair Lewis   91
Now Ameriky *by* Betty Sue Cummings   92
The Other Shore *by* Lucinda Mays   93
The Pit: A Story of Chicago *by* Frank Norris   93
Ragtime *by* E. L. Doctorow   94
The Rise of David Levinsky *by* Abraham Cahan   95
Sister Carrie *by* Theodore Dreiser   96
The Sport of the Gods *by* Paul Laurence Dunbar   97
Streets of Gold *by* Karen Branson   98
The Tempering *by* Gloria Skurzynski   98
Voyage *by* Adele Geras   99

VI.   THE JAZZ AGE AND THE DEPRESSION   101

All the King's Men *by* Robert Penn Warren   101
Appointment in Samarra *by* John O'Hara   102
Circle of Fire *by* William H. Hooks   102
The Dark Didn't Catch Me *by* Crystal Thrasher   103
A Girl Named Sooner *by* Suzanne Clauser   104
The Grapes of Wrath *by* John Steinbeck   104
The Great Gatsby *by* F. Scott Fitzgerald   105
King of the Hill *by* A. E. Hotchner   106
Let the Circle Be Unbroken *by* Mildred D. Taylor   107

Manhattan Transfer *by* John Dos Passos   108
Native Son *by* Richard Wright   108
No Promises in the Wind *by* Irene Hunt   109
The Rock and the Willow *by* Mildred Lee   110
Roll of Thunder, Hear My Cry *by* Mildred D. Taylor   111
Tracks *by* Clayton Bess   111
Walk Gently This Good Earth *by* Margaret Craven   112

VII. AMERICA IN THE MODERN WORLD   115

Alan and Naomi *by* Myron Levoy   115
The Bridges at Toko-ri *by* James A. Michener   116
Caribou *by* Meg Wolitzer   116
The Dollmaker *by* Harriette Arnow   117
Fallen Angels *by* Walter Dean Myers   118
Fragments *by* Jack Fuller   119
Freedom's Blood *by* James D. Foreman   120
Going after Cacciato *by* Tim O'Brien   120
Invisible Man *by* Ralph Ellison   121
Journey Home *by* Yoshiko Uchida   122
Journey to Topaz *by* Yoshiko Uchida   123
The Last Mission *by* Harry Mazer   123
A Necessary End *by* Nathaniel Benchley   124
One More Time *by* Charles Ferry   125
Pageant *by* Kathryn Lasky   126
Raspberry One *by* Charles Ferry   127
Rumors of Peace *by* Ella Leffland   128
Summer of My German Soldier *by* Bette Greene   128
To Stand against the Wind
    by Ann Nolan Clark   129
A Woman of Independent Means *by*
    Elizabeth Forsythe Hailey   130

AUTHOR-TITLE INDEX   133

INTRODUCTION

THE NEED

"History is so-o-o bo-o-o-ring!"

"Why do we have to learn about these old battles anyway?"

"Who cares about the Treaty of Guadeloupe Hidalgo?"

There is growing awareness being voiced both in the literature of education and in the general press that today's graduates of American high schools have little knowledge and less understanding of their country's past. Although they occupy seats in American history class, trudge through their textbooks, and generally pass their tests, they have not learned very much. They have crammed in elections and generals and treaties—why? To get through the exam. That's history. A trivial pursuit. Now it's over, and so what? Too soon it's all forgotten.

Of course, social studies teachers are concerned. Although they certainly want their students to succeed in the Regents or the College Boards, their goals are far broader. Teachers hope that students will develop a critical sense, a spirit of inquiry. They want them to acquire historical understanding, and even enthusiasm.

But how?

A SOLUTION

The suggestion here is, try historical fiction *first*.

What is needed is an antidote to combat the widespread disinterest in and lack of excitement about the study of American history. Students need to see that history is alive. This will happen when they are able to think of history first of all as story. And students must discover that the key actors in the story are ordinary people doing, for the most part, what ordinary people do, and feeling what ordinary people feel. Then students can realize that they, too, are part of the story. This analytical handbook of American historical fiction is designed to help social studies teachers and school librarians turn students on to history through story.

THE TEXTBOOKS

Of course, the textbook will continue to be the foundation for teaching American history. But despite continuing improvements in textbooks—greater visual appeal, more excerpts from primary documents, more human interest inserts—most students find textbooks boring. Frances Fitzgerald, in her study of American history texts, suggests a reason. Current publishing guidelines allow little freedom to individual authors, so that textbooks tend to be the product of panels or committees, and thus relatively sterile (*America Revised: History Schoolbooks in the Twentieth Century.* Boston: Little, Brown, 1979. p. 69). Another reason, suggested by some critics, is that contemporary historiography, which tends to use non-narrative techniques, has deliberately downplayed the role of story. The result? Textbooks are "boring."

But by reading historical fiction in conjunction with the textbook, students may yet come to see history as the story of real people with feelings, values, needs to which they themselves can relate, based on their own experiences and interests. This feeling of connection or relatedness, of participation in the story, is crucial for students. The present volume addresses this crucial need.

STARTING WITH STORY

Of course, from time to time many teachers do assign historical fiction. *Johnny Tremain, Uncle Tom's Cabin,* and a number of other familiar titles appear on many lists of suggested reading. But the reading of novels has been considered largely a supplementary or even optional activity. To revitalize the study of history, fiction can play an important role.

So, start with story. It is recommended that teachers consider assigning an appropriate novel (or novels) at the beginning of each new unit. By plunging vicariously into the experiences of fictional young people, building a sod house on the Nebraska prairie, following the North Star with a bold band of escaping slaves, or parachuting into enemy territory after a B-17 is shot down, students will find history coming to life. The hard data in the textbook will have more meaning. And students will then be able to contribute to class discussions lively insights derived from their individual reading.

Through this method of revitalizing history, it is expected that junior/middle and high school students will develop increased comprehension of their country's past. Once students begin to see history as story, and related to the destinies of "ordinary" people like themselves, teachers may then find it possible to lead them to develop that critical sense and spirit of inquiry so important for real understanding. Some may ultimately be led to read historical fiction for pleasure as well.

THIS BOOK

The 154 books in this annotated compilation have been selected and arranged to present aspects of American history through story. While historical events, such as Civil War battles, are important to the content in many of the books, in others, the emphasis is on the lives of ordinary people living ordinary lives in an historical context. It is this idea, that history is the story of individual lives, which is considered most important for students to comprehend.

The books are arranged in seven broad chronological/topical categories. Within each category they are listed alphabetically by title. An author-title index is provided.

The following guidelines were used in the selection of books. All were published after 1900, and most within the last twenty years.

1. *Time and place.* The time period covered in these books ranges from the beginning of the colonial era in the late 1500s to the post-Vietnam War era of the 1970s. The setting is what is now the United States (except for a few dealing with immigration or with United States wars in the twentieth century, where the action takes place in Europe or Asia).

2. *Reading level.* The symbol *(1)* following the citation indicates books recommended for upper-level students (grades 11–12); the symbol *(2)* indicates a mid-range (grades 9–10); and the symbol *(3)* denotes books at the junior high or middle school level (grades 6–8). It is understood that students in any given grade may be reading at any of these levels. The symbols are provided to guide the teacher or librarian in recommending books to individual students.

3. *Quality.* Historical fiction in the style of potboiling romances or swashbuckling adventure tales has not been included. This handbook focuses on books of literary quality which present not only history carefully researched and accurately recounted but also characters with whom young readers can identify, and situations which provide for thoughtful involvement. Most were drawn from respected bibliographies of recommended books; others were suggested by knowledgeable experts in the field of American history.

4. *Content of entry.* Each entry contains three parts. First, there is a short annotation introducing the plot. Although the volume is intended primarily for teachers and librarians, the annotations are designed to arouse interest and may be used to promote the books with prospective readers. A second paragraph provides a comment on historicity, i.e., an indication of what a student might learn about historical events or the ways of living, customs, attitudes, and values of the time. (Instances of sexual explicitness and strong language are noted in books for younger readers.) The third part, Suggestions for Reports or Activities, lists some ideas for possible follow-up to the

reading. At least one question or activity is based on historical events described or referred to in the story; others may deal with historical, literary, or affective considerations. But these are suggestions only. It is expected that teachers, librarians, and students will devise additional follow-up activities.

ARRANGEMENT BY HISTORICAL PERIODS

I. *Colonial America*. This period stretches from the late sixteenth century when Europeans initially began to settle the New World until the early 1770s. Books in this section deal with such topics as the disappearance of the Roanoke colony, the growth of Plymouth, the Puritans and their way of life, the Salem witch trials, settlement of North Carolina by the Huguenots, and early relationships with the Indians. Several portray how young whites captured by the Indians grew to prefer their new lives.

II. *The American Revolution and the New Nation*. The novels in this section take place in the period beginning in the mid-1770s, when the tensions peaked between the British government and the colonists, through the American Revolution and the ratification of the Constitution, to the early days of the new nation. Readers will learn of contrasting views of loyalists and self-styled patriots. The unglamorous aspects of war are described through accounts of the winter at Valley Forge, or the tarring and feathering of a Tory sympathizer by a Patriot mob. Other topics include Shays' Rebellion and conflicts over land grants between Connecticut and Pennsylvania settlers.

III. *The Civil War and Reconstruction*. Books in this period take place generally from the 1830s through the 1870s. Exceptions include some "chronicles" whose most important action takes place during the Civil War, but which may begin earlier, and/or extend beyond the Reconstruction period. Books dealing with the issue of slavery, life in the South, the Underground Railroad, the action of the war, and Reconstruction are annotated. There are some books written from a slave's point of view.

IV. *Westward Expansion and the Native American Response*. The westward movement in its varied aspects provides rich materials for novelists. The period covered is the nineteenth century until the closing of the frontier. Included are the explorations of Lewis and Clark, glimpses of the ruggedness of pioneer life, frontier justice, and portrayals of conflicts with the Indians. Current fiction reflects changing attitudes toward Native Americans, conveying appreciation for Indian peoples and culture and acknowledgment of wrongdoing on the part of the newcomers.

V. *Immigration, Industrialization, Urbanization*. These books are set in the period from the mid-nineteenth century through World War I. The inter-related topics cover also the rise of the new-moneyed class, and the "Gilded Age." The hardships for immigrants aboard ship and the struggle to find the elusive "streets of gold" are described. Included in this section are several classics of American literature.

VI. *The Jazz Age and the Depression*. The period covered extends from 1918 through the 1930s. Books set in the 1920s depict the life of the leisure class and the "Jazz Age." Themes in the 1930s revolve around the Great Depression and the plight of blacks in the era of Jim Crow.

VII. *America in the Modern World*. This period begins in the 1940s and extends to the post-Vietnam War era. World War II novels include descriptions of the close-knit, fragile community of a crew aboard a B-17 bomber, the detention of Japanese-Americans in U.S. internment camps, and the psychological effect of the horrors of war on a young Jewish refugee. One novel for younger readers describes a family's reaction to a member who chooses to go to Canada rather than to Vietnam. Another from the point of view of a young Vietnamese immigrant to America recalls the pain the war brought to his family.

ACKNOWLEDGMENTS

The following bibliographies were consulted for selecting books to be included in this volume: the H. W. Wilson *Senior High School Catalog,* and *Junior High School Catalog; The American History Book List for High Schools* (National Council for the Social Studies, 1971); the National Council of Teachers of English (NCTE) lists for junior and senior high schools; and the New York Public Library's *Books for the Teen Age.* Other helpful resources were Lillian Shapiro's *Fiction for Youth,* 2nd ed. (Neal-Schuman, 1986); Elinor Walker's *Doors to More Mature Reading* (2nd ed., ALA, 1981); and Alleen Nilsen and Ken Donelson's *Literature for Today's Young Adults,* 2nd ed. (Scott, Foresman, 1985).

The lists of "Notable Trade Books in the Social Studies" found annually in the April issue of *Social Education* were useful for junior high/middle school books. The American Library Association list of young adult books, *The Best of the Best, 1970–1982,* yielded some important titles. Recommended books were also located through reviews in *Horn Book Magazine, School Library Journal,* and *Bulletin of the Center for Children's Books.*

Additional titles were recommended by such experts as Professor Otey M. Scruggs, American history specialist and chairman of the Department of History at Syracuse University, and Barbara Elam, coordinator of school libraries for the Boston Public Schools. Other educators around the country who responded most generously to requests for advice or suggestions included the following: J. Kenneth Bradford, associate director, English, Language Arts and Reading, Virginia; Ann Symons, Department of Education, Alaska; Larry N. Strickland, supervisor, Social Studies, Washington (state); Elaine M. Takenaka, Department of Education, Hawaii; H. Michael Hartoonian, Social Studies supervisor, Wisconsin; Harry Stein, Social Studies and Basic Skills consultant, Department of Education, New Jersey; Ronald V. Sartor, executive director, Michigan Council for the Social Studies; Carol H. Sill, Los Altos High School, California; Mary McFarland, instructional coordinator of Social Studies, Parkway School District, Chesterfield, Missouri; Richard Kraft, member, Board of Directors, National Council for the Social Studies, Washington, D.C.; Donald O. Schneider, College of Education, University of Georgia, Athens, Georgia, and president, National Council for the Social Studies; and Bert Cieslak, National Council for the Social Studies, Washington, D.C.

xvii

Books were read by the author or a member of the review panel, which consisted of Rosemary Coffey, M.A., curriculum specialist, Pittsburgh Public Schools; Susan Taylor, Ph.D., supervisory instructional specialist, Pittsburgh Public Schools; and Otey M. Scruggs, Ph.D., chairman, Department of History, Syracuse University. Rosemary Coffey deserves special note for her contributions to the annotations of books for older readers. Additional valuable assistance was rendered by Mary Hales Smith, English and library science student, West Virginia University, and Barbara F. Scruggs, former English teacher, Santa Barbara, California, public schools.

The encouragement, confidence, and good counsel of Herbert Bloom, senior editor, ALA Books, made it possible for the project to come to life.

Unstinting aid was consistently and joyously provided by Lawrence C. Howard, adviser, consoler, word processing whiz, husband, and friend. The book would never have been finished without his constant gentle prodding.

To all of the above, sincerest gratitude.

ELIZABETH FITZGERALD HOWARD

I

COLONIAL AMERICA

Calico Bush, by Rachel Field.
New York: Macmillan, 1931. 201p. (3)

It seems hard to believe that only a year ago she was in her beloved France, happy and loved. Now everything is changed, even her name. The delicate Marguerite Ledoux, who loved to dance and could sew fancy little stitches, is now Maggie, the Sargents' bound-out servant. Marguerite, Grand'mère and Uncle set sail for America with hopes for a shiny new future. But Uncle died, and then Grand'mère's illness and subsequent death left Marguerite a penniless orphan. The Sargent family took her in, and now they are moving to the wilderness of Maine. Maggie is brave and resourceful, gets along well with the children, and is eager to please. The family is ill-prepared for frontier life and faces many dangers. Hostile Indians and wild animals are tough foes, but the bitter cold is even harder to bear. Although hardship and tragedy mark Maggie's thirteenth year, her trials strengthen her as she begins to grow toward womanhood.

Comment

Details such as the breaking of sod to plant crops and the weaving of cloth to make clothing make this portrayal of the early American frontier realistic. Maggie's experience with anti-French prejudice is informative: the clash between English and French settlers led to eventual war. Readers will gain a real sense of what it meant to leave "civilization" to settle in a wilderness area.

Suggestions for Reports or Activities

1. Imagine that you are going to move to an unsettled wilderness region such as Marguerite had to do. You can take only ten items. Decide what to take and give a rationale for your choices.

2. Consider the items that the Sargents decided to take to Maine. Write a rationale explaining the wisdom or ignorance that they exhibited in deciding to transport those specific items.

3. Find out what you can about the early settlement of Maine. Compare your discoveries with the information provided in the novel.

4. What were the reasons for anti-French prejudice?

Calico Captive, by Elizabeth George Speare.
Boston: Houghton Mifflin, 1957. 274p. (3)

At her very first dancing party Miriam discovers that she and Phineas Whitney have a bond between them, but the next morning her whole world is changed. Indians attack her family's cabin. Miriam, along with her sister Susanna, her brother-in-law James, and their children, are captured, and forced to march toward an uncertain fate. Miriam is terrified but learns that the Indians do not intend to harm them. Rather, they will most likely be sold to the French. Susanna gives birth to a baby girl, whom she names Captive, and has to stay behind with the Indians. Miriam is transported north to become a servant in a wealthy French home in Montreal. There she meets dashing, romantic Pierre who almost makes her forget Phineas Whitney.

Comment

This book is an interesting look at the tensions building up between the English and the French over land rights in North America. Readers will become aware of Indian-French cooperation against the English, including the Indian practice of capturing English settlers and selling them to the French. Montreal is described as a cultured, urbane place. This book is valuable in casting some light on the fact that Canadian history is connected to U.S. history.

Suggestions for Reports or Activities

1. What were the causes of the French and Indian Wars? What was the conclusion?

2. The story is based on actual fact. English settlers were captured by the Indians and sold to the French. Can you find any more information about this practice in a reference source?

3. At the end of the story Miriam thinks that New Englanders believe that Montreal is a "place of wickedness, like the ancient cities of Sodom and Gomorrah." Why would the New England colonists have such an opinion?

Constance: A Story of Early Plymouth, by Patricia Clapp.
New York: Lothrop, Lee & Shepard, 1968. 255p. (2,3)

From the moment land is first sighted from the *Mayflower* Constance Hopkins is determined to hate America. In her journal she records the fear and excitement of landing and beginning to build the Plymouth community, the sparsely furnished cabin she must now call home, the tentative friendship with nearby Indians, the terrible sickness which in those first months took the lives of half of the brave band. She describes the cold, the drought, the hunger, and the anguish of the loss of loved ones. But she records the good times, too—the joy in the times of plenty, the feasting, and the flirting. This is a lively account of an adolescent's concern for herself and her concern for her relationships with others: father, stepmother, and the young men who take an interest in her. Constance gradually accepts this strange new place.

Comment

The formidable task of eking out a living from the barren shores of New England is realistically portrayed. Within the context of a very engaging story Clapp provides readers with solid historical background on topics such as the agreement between the *Mayflower* group and their sponsors which led to the establishment of the Plymouth colony, changing methods of government and land allotment, the diversity of the group (not all were members of the church), the peaceful trading with the Indians, the means of disciplining people who did not follow the rules of the community. Through the reflections of Constance, fourteen years old in the beginning, and twenty at the end, the growing pains of Plymouth and those of a high-spirited maturing young adult are intertwined.

Suggestions for Reports or Activities

1. What can you discover in the book about the reasons for the establishment of the Plymouth colony?

2. What was the role of women at Plymouth? Did they play any part in making policy for the colony?

3. People from different cultures have often complained about how other people look, dress, smell, talk, and so forth. Can you think of some instances today where some people are bothered by personal or physical attributes of others? What can you say about the value of discussing this point?

A Country of Strangers, by Conrad Richter.
New York: Knopf, 1966. 169p. (3)

Fifteen-year-old Stone Girl, once known as Mary Stanton, reluctantly leaves her Indian husband and flees to another Ohio village with her young son. This seems to be her only chance to avoid being returned to the white family from which she was kidnapped ten years earlier and which she scarcely remembers. When her husband fails to come after her, Stone Girl is ultimately led to her father's home. However, Captain Stanton refuses to accept her, and she has come too far from her Indian village to return by herself. Her dilemma is resolved only after the death of her son, Otter Boy.

Comment

Told from the point of view of a young white woman who wants to stay with the Indians, this story offers an unusual perspective on the terrible experience suffered by many settlers on the frontier, namely, losing a child to the alien and greatly feared Indians whose land they had appropriated. By articulating the emotional ties which many of these children developed with their captors, the author makes plausible the idea that not all were glad to return to their families and to the white way of life.

Suggestions for Reports or Activities

1. Check some of the historical accounts of the colonial period in Ohio and Pennsylvania for information on the Indians' return of their white captives. Are there any details of real children who were reluctant to go back?

2. Imagine the history of the other girl who claimed to be Mary Stanton. Who was she? Where did she come from? How did she manage to persuade Captain Stanton that she was his real daughter?

3. Think about Captain Stanton's reasons for refusing to recognize Stone Girl as his daughter. How valid were they? Could you have countered his arguments any better than his mother did? What would you have said?

The Forest and the Fort, by Hervey Allen.
New York: Rinehart, 1943. 344p. (2)

Salathiel Albine, a white youngster who has lived as Little Turtle with the Shawnee Indians from the age of four or five, chooses to reidentify with his white parentage after spending some time with a preacher who helps him relearn English. Sal finds himself engaged as a personal manservant to Captain Simeon Bouyer, who is charged with protecting Fort Pitt from Indian attack and bolstering Forts Ligonier and Bedford farther east. Entrusted with increasing authority, Sal appreciates his expanded opportunities and looks forward to further adventures.

Comment

Narrated in a leisurely style, this tale offers an account of a young man stolen by the Indians who makes a successful readjustment to white civilization. The contrasts between the lives he led as Little Turtle and as Salathiel Albine point up the cultural differences which made Indian-white conflict, particularly regarding proper use of the land, virtually inevitable as the settlers pressed westward.

Suggestions for Reports or Activities

1. Check the historical accounts of the battle of Fort Pitt. How close are they to Allen's version? What differences are there, if any? Why do you suppose Allen made changes (if he did)?

2. Simeon Bouyer and Henry Bouquet were real persons. Find out something about their lives. Why did they come to America? What happened to them after the battles described in this book?

3. Imagine yourself as Little Turtle's mother or father. Why did the mother start drinking a lot? Why did the father not try to keep Little Turtle with him? Write down the thoughts of one of them as she or he became aware that Little Turtle would be returning to his people.

The Light in the Forest, by Conrad Richter.
New York: Knopf, 1953. 117p. (3)

True Son is angry. As part of an agreement to keep peace, whites are insisting that captives who have been living with the Indians be returned to their white settlements. True Son, fifteen years old, has lived with the Delaware tribe since being captured as a baby. He resents his real parents and the alien ways of whites: their strange smell, restrictive clothing, tasteless food. But he grows to love his little brother, Gordie. However, some of his relatives have had unhappy experiences with Indians, and nurse a deep hatred. When Little Crane is found murdered by True Son's uncle, True Son decides to return to his Indian family. While taking part in an retaliatory ambush, he realizes that his loyalties are split. Where does True Son belong?

Comment

Although True Son was born into a white family, his point of view is Indian. Historical records show that many white captives preferred to remain with the Indians. By emphasizing True Son's identification with his Indian captors, the author provides readers an alternate view of colonial society, and encourages the appreciation of Indian culture. He makes clear that to the Indians the Europeans were the barbarians, a view which Europeans could not even imagine.

Suggestions for Reports or Activities

1. Check into some actual accounts of whites who were captured by the Indians and became acclimated to Indian ways, preferring to stay with the Indians. Write a short paper about one of these people.

2. What are some of the comparisons True Son made between the life of the Indians and the life of the white settlers? Write an imaginary letter from True Son to his biological parents explaining why he does not wish to return to them.

3. Find out about relationships between the Indians of Pennsylvania and the early settlers. How did the Quakers, Pennsylvania's first European settlers, regard the Indians?

Lusty Wind for Carolina, by Inglis Fletcher.
New York: Bobbs-Merrill, 1944. 509p. (1)

French Huguenot weaver Robert Fountaine and his family are the main characters of this story. Settling on the Cape Fear River by the North Carolina coast, the Fountaines hope to build a new life in the New World, safe at last from the religious persecution they had known in the Old. Along with their fellow settlers from Bristol, England, they confront the unknown elements of Carolina: Indians, hurricanes, long-distance governance from England, planters already divided into political factions, pirates, and their own disappointments.

Comment

Noting the determination of the settlers to develop their own products and maintain free trade routes from the American plantations to world markets, the book places the story of the settlers against the wider backdrop of pirate control of much of the Caribbean and the long outer banks flanking the coast of Carolina. At times, the pirates themselves are the focus of the action. Romantic and political intrigues link the fictional and the historical characters throughout.

Suggestions for Reports or Activities

1. A number of the pirates featured in this book were real people: Anne Bonney, Jack Rackham, Edward Teach (''Blackbeard''), Stede Bonnet. See what you can find out about their lives and their reasons for turning to piracy.

2. Mention is made of the two previous settlements on the Cape Fear River. When were they founded? What happened to them?

3. Who were the French Huguenots? Why were they persecuted? Where were they living originally and where did they go?

4. Why did many of the supporters of the Duke of Monmouth (''the Pretender'') end up as bondsmen? What did it mean to be a ''Jacobin''?

Mercy Short: A Winter Journal, North Boston, 1692-93, by Norma Farber.
New York: Dutton, 1982. 138p. (2, 3)

When her family was massacred in an Indian raid, fifteen-year-old Mercy was taken captive and lived most of a year in an Indian village. Now, after two years as an indentured servant with a family in Boston, Mercy seems plagued by memories of her experience. The young Reverend Cotton Mather, with a reputation for exorcism, is trying to cure her of what he says are demons. He suggests that Mercy keep a journal to record her bouts with the devil. In her journal Mercy tells of the massacre, of the forced march, and of her life. But her reminiscences of the Indians are largely gentle; she records with tenderness giving birth to a short-lived half-Indian child. After some months of recording what Reverend Mather directs, Mercy seems to be cured, but she can see devils when she thinks Reverend Mather wants her to. However, she knows she must appear well, now that the handsome chorister with corn-flower blue eyes is seeking permission to court her.

Comment

The author has developed Mercy's story from a few lines about her in the writings of Cotton Mather, noted minister from Puritan Boston. Included are lively descriptions of the bustling seaport of Boston, absorbing details of routines (housekeeping, food preparation, clothing, worship, courtship) and of the restrictive Puritan code (no merrymaking, no dancing, no celebration at Christmas, endless hours in church, constant reflection on sin, and so forth). Mercy records her appreciation of the wisdom and ways of the Indians who captured her, comparing them with the presumably more civilized English settlers. There is a forceful picture of the zealous Reverend Mather. Readers will empathize with a young woman who is trying to find a place for herself, questioning her own English and Christian civilization for its ideas on Indians, slaves, and religious practices.

Suggestions for Reports or Activities

1. Who was Cotton Mather? What were his contributions to the cultural and religious life of his time? What can you find out about his interests in science and medicine?

2. Mercy states that some of the colonists who were captured by the Indians came to prefer Indian life to their own. Can you find any evidence for this statement?

3. The Salem witch trials are mentioned in this story. Do you think the reports from Salem influenced either Mercy or Cotton Mather? Explain.

4. Mercy reads some poetry by Anne Bradstreet. Who was she?

Roanoke: A Novel of the Lost Colony, by Sonia Levitin.
New York: Atheneum, 1973. 213p. (3)

To escape his cruel master, orphan William Wythers decides to leave England. He becomes a colonist headed for adventure in the New World. To his dismay, the voyage is miserable, the captain dishonest and cruel, and the colonists disorganized and argumentative. They are forced by the captain to land in Roanoke, Virginia, instead of Chesapeake. William befriends and learns from the Indians and eventually falls in love. When the colony is attacked and massacred, William is saved by his new friends.

Comment

The Roanoke colonists became one of America's early mysteries when all traces of them disappeared. The main historical facts as portrayed in this book are accurate. They are woven into a believable narrative about what life might have been for the lost colony. The settlers' attitudes toward the native "savages," the disease and barbaric treatment brought by the colonists themselves, and the greed, death, and suffering marking that first winter are described.

Suggestions for Reports or Activities

1. Research information about the lost colony. What are some of the explanations given for its disappearance? How do these explanations fit with the one offered by the book?

2. We are told about William's letter to his nine-year-old sister Bessie, who is still in London, but we do not read his text. Write William's letter, telling Bessie about the New World in a positive way.

3. *Roanoke* is told from William's point of view. However, the Indians were already settled in the area when the colonists arrived. Why did one tribe react in a friendly manner while the other one attacked? How did they accept the colonists' God?

The Sign of the Beaver, by Elizabeth George Speare. Boston: Houghton Mifflin, 1983. 135p. (3)

Matt and his father have finished building their cabin in the Maine wilderness. Now Matt will be alone for about six weeks, guarding the house and weeding the garden while waiting for his father to return with his mother and sister and the new baby. Matt is apprehensive, but he manages well, even after a wily stranger steals his gun. When a bear ransacks the cabin, food is scarce, but Matt is resourceful. However, trying to get honey, Matt is attacked by bees and nearly dies. He is helped by Attean and his grandfather, from a nearby Indian tribe. Attean's grandfather decides that Matt will teach Attean to read in return for being supplied with enough rabbits and squirrels to eat. The boys are reluctant at first, but after a while a close friendship develops. Parting is painful for both of them.

Comment

This story is full of information on living as newcomers to the American wilderness learned to do. The kinds of responsibilities which young people in colonial America were expected to assume are shown in the task which Matt's father leaves with him. Attean's communication of Indian ideas (sharing the land, killing game only for food, respecting others, carefully using the gifts of the forest) and his comments on the white settlers' killing his parents afford today's readers an opportunity to consider the westward movement from an Indian point of view.

Suggestions for Reports or Activities

1. What did Matt learn from Attean? After you have considered some of the survival skills which Attean taught Matt, consider the Indians' values that Matt learned. How were some of these ideas and values communicated to Matt?

2. Matt's new house was in Maine. His old house was in Quincy, Massachusetts. Look at a map of New England. Pick a possible location in Maine for Matt's cabin. What present-day cities lie along the road that went through the wilderness to Maine? Did any of these towns already exist in Matt's time?

The Stratford Devil, by Claude Clayton Smith.
New York: Walker, 1984. 192p. (2, 3)

Ruth Paine, adopted daughter of an elderly widow, is different from the other girls in Stratford, Connecticut, in the middle of the seventeenth century. She is more inquisitive, more independent, and braver, as well. From the age of twelve, when she has an adventure with wolves and local Indians— both greatly feared by the townspeople—to her brutal and sudden death at twenty-three, Ruth goes her own way. She dies, deserted by the father she has just come to know and made a scapegoat by people who did not understand, and thus disliked her.

Comment

Basing his story on a true happening (the hanging of a young woman as a witch in Stratford nearly fifty years before the famous witch trials in Salem, Massachusetts), the author creates a cast of characters and a series of incidents to illustrate how this unusual circumstance might have come about. As the plot develops, the reader comes to a greater understanding of the values and motivations of the Puritans, their relationships with neighboring Indians, and their fear of the world of nature.

Suggestions for Reports or Activities

1. From a careful reading of this book, select the values that appear to govern the Stratford Puritans. How do these resemble, or differ from, the values of a contemporary religious group of your choice?

2. Why was it so important to the Widow Paine that the townspeople believe she was the biological mother of Ruth?

3. Reconstruct the incidents that led Stratford to accuse Ruth of witchcraft. Why did she not defend herself? Why did she "confess" in the end?

4. Research the relationship of the Stratford residents and the Indians in the surrounding area during the first part of the seventeenth century. What happened?

Tituba of Salem Village, by Ann Petry.
New York: Crowell, 1964. 254p. (2, 3)

Slaves in Barbados, Tituba and her husband John are suddenly sold to a minister, who moves to Salem Village. There Tituba cares for the minister's invalid wife, daughter, and niece. Salem Village proves to be cold and dismal, and Tituba's master greedy and self-seeking. Tituba, too capable at her duties and not fitting the community's standards, eventually is accused of witchcraft by the niece and others of the village girls. Tituba and two other women are proclaimed to be witches, suffer through a trial, and are then imprisoned.

Comment
Petry has captured the hysteria and fear surrounding the witch trials. She builds the evidence against Tituba in such a clear, logical manner that the reader empathizes with and fears for Tituba. At the same time, Petry realistically pictures a struggling community that can accept success or difference only as the result of an alliance with the devil. The unfairness of the trial is frustrating to the modern reader even as it reflects the tone and mood of the times.

Suggestions for Reports or Activities
1. Tituba, Sarah Good, Sarah Osburne, and others were brought to trial on charges of witchcraft. What happened to these people? Where did Tituba go? Who were the other people involved?

2. Who were some of the famous judges who presided in the Salem witch trials? Why do you think they believed that the accused were witches?

3. Write a journal from Abigail's point of view. Why would she accuse Tituba of witchcraft? What are Abigail's feelings during the trial?

4. Draw a map depicting Tituba's journey from Barbados to Boston and then to Salem Village. Note the various means of transportation that she used.

The Witch of Blackbird Pond, by Elizabeth George Speare.
Boston: Houghton Mifflin, 1958. 249p. (3)

Adjusting to the strict and solemn ways of Puritan Connecticut is difficult for Kit, who has grown up in the easygoing life of high-church Barbados. But her cousins Mercy and Judith are welcoming and friendly, and there are some interesting young men. Kit learns to be useful with the endless household tasks, and joins Mercy in conducting a dame school. Despite her uncle's prohibition, she persists in her friendship with Hannah Tupper, the Quaker outcast whom the townspeople have declared a witch. She also manages some secret reading lessons for little Prudence who has been thought too backward to learn. But then comes the sickness and with it the fear that witchcraft is the cause. In an exciting rescue, Kit manages to get Hannah to safety, but Kit is forced to stand trial.

Comment

Life in a small New England town in the time of Puritan dominance is serious. But readers will also discover that the colonists were quite human. There are rich details of daily life, such as the meager meals, styles of dress, religious practices, schools, courtship patterns, and ways of healing the sick. This picture of the prevailing attitudes is compelling: the demand for conformity and suspicion of people who were different. Kit's audaciousness and Hannah Tupper's fortitude are in sharp contrast to accepted patterns of behavior.

Suggestions for Reports or Activities

1. How are Kit and Hannah Tupper alike? Describe how they were treated by the people of Wethersfield. What can you learn about the early colonists' attitudes toward people who were different? Can you suggest any reasons for these attitudes?

2. The people of Connecticut were concerned about their charter from the king. Find out about this charter. What rights were granted to the settlers. Why were they worried?

3. This book describes many of the activities and practices in the day-to-day lives of Kit and her Connecticut cousins. Select one of these activities, such as preparation of meals, making of clothing, caring for the sick, educating the children, worshipping God. Research your topic. Prepare an oral report for class.

4. Why was Wethersfield an important settlement?

Witches' Children: A Story of Salem, by Patricia Clapp.
New York: Lothrop, Lee & Shepard, 1982. 160p. (1, 2, 3)

Told years later from the point of view of Mary Warren, who had been a bound girl in the house of John and Elizabeth Proctor, this strange and sad tale of fear, superstition, terror, and skewed justice unfolds. Mary notes that Tituba, the slave from Barbados, had been reading palms and foretold that something frightening would take place. Abigail Parris, who had been complaining about her boring life, begins to have screaming fits, and other girls, including Mary, follow her lead. The villagers believe that the girls are possessed by the devil and that the devil must have helpers. Tituba and two other women are arrested as witches, and as the fits continue many other persons are accused. Those who, under lengthy questioning, confess that they are witches are exonerated, but before the madness ends, twenty people are put to death.

Comment

This is a gripping story of the Salem witch trials and the circumstances that precipitated them, the hysteria of several young girls and the superstition and ignorance of the adults who could not understand what was happening. The pressure on the girls to name "witches," and on the accused to confess that they were guilty as well as the use of "spectral evidence" in the trials all afford a view of the Puritan theocratic system of justice. The story also provides a picture of daily life and work (such as farming, food preparation, making of clothing, managing an inn) in a colonial town.

Suggestions for Reports or Activities

1. Check in an encyclopedia or other source for additional information about the reasons for the Salem witch trials, and the outcome. Discuss how accurately the author has reported.

2. Write a newspaper article describing the events in the story. Whom would you interview? How would their stories differ?

3. What do you think is Tituba's role in the affair? Do you believe that she bears any responsibility for what happened? Explain.

4. Try to assess the responsibility for the witch trials, listing the people, the events, and the beliefs that helped to force the situation. Assign a value to each item you list: very important, somewhat important, not very important.

II

THE AMERICAN REVOLUTION AND THE NEW NATION

April Morning, by Howard Fast.
New York: Crown, 1961. 184p. (3)

Adam Cooper has a little brother who annoys him and a father who fails to appreciate him. Still a boy at fifteen, yet yearning to be a man, Adam dares to sign the muster roll of the Lexington militia on April 19, 1775. His father, although surprised, does not interfere. Thus Adam is standing with the rest of the local farmers and shopkeepers when the British army marches by on its way to Concord, where the ammunition is said to be stored.

Comment

Told from the point of view of a boy who has to become a man in a matter of hours, the story emphasizes the astonishment of the Massachusetts farmers at finding themselves suddenly at war with the British. Made vivid and authentic for the reader are: Adam's outrage at the British decision to fire; his agony at seeing his father die; his disillusionment at the powerlessness of words when confronted with bullets; and his maturation in the course of the rest of the events of that long and memorable day.

Suggestions for Reports or Activities

1. Try to find a British account of the Battle of Lexington. Why did the British fire at men whose guns weren't even cocked? What were their orders? What happened to the British later at Concord? How many made it back to Boston?

2. Read Henry Wadsworth Longfellow's narrative poem ''Paul Revere's Ride.'' Could Revere have been the one who alerted the Lexington farmers? What does the poem say about what happened afterwards? Compare Longfellow's account with Fast's.

3. Imagine the battle and the other events of the day from the point of view of Levi, Adam's little brother. How much did he see? How much could he only guess at? Write an entry from Levi's journal telling his reactions.

Arundel, by Kenneth Roberts.
Garden City, N.Y.: Doubleday, 1933. 486p. (1)
Steven Nason, young innkeeper in Arundel, Maine, is the chief protagonist of this novel. Through Steven, we take part in the first stirring of independence in the colonies and come to know such figures of early American history as Benedict Arnold and Aaron Burr. Steven tells us of the terrible journey made by Colonel Arnold and his soldiers through the Maine wilderness to Quebec in a vain attempt to dislodge the British, many months before the Declaration of Independence. Provocative relationships among the fictional characters are developed as a counterpoint to the historical themes.

Comment
The author describes the vital role played by the Abenaki Indians and other tribes in facilitating the journey of the American soldiers. Although many sickened and died on the trek through the swamps and the forests, casualties would have been much higher without the help of the Indians. Also significant is the depiction of Benedict Arnold, known to most students as a traitor, as an inspired and vocal leader.

Suggestions for Reports or Activities
1. Find Arnold's account (chapter 14) of his relations with Ethan Allen and the Green Mountain Boys at Ticonderoga. How does it compare with other versions in your history text or in an encyclopedia?
2. The Mary Mallinson whom Steven remembered as a little girl was very different from the Marie de Sabrevois whom he found in Quebec. Explain what might have happened to Mary after her kidnapping to change her so much.
3. The soldiers from the various states tended to be suspicious of each other. With Steven and the Indian Natanis as models, tell what might need to happen for these men to begin to think of each other as "brothers."

The Bloody Country, by James Lincoln Collier
and Christopher Collier.
New York: Macmillan, 1976. 181p. (2, 3)
Ben Buck tells this story of his father's stubborn determination to find his own life in the Pennsylvania wilderness. Not enough people are planting grain to keep their mill busy, but Daniel Buck refuses to be forced to live as

a hired man on his brother's Connecticut farm. So he accepts a good offer of a mill and some acreage 200 miles west near Wilkes-Barre, Pennsylvania. But this land is part of a disputed grant, fought over by Connecticut settlers and Pennsylvanians. Indians, British soldiers, and Tories join in cruel tactics to drive out the newcomers, but Ben's father refuses to leave, even after his wife and son-in-law are massacred. Throughout the story Ben has a difficult time trying to reconcile his father's passion for freedom to live his own life with his equally passionate inability to consider freedom for Joe Mountain, the half-Indian half-black youth whom he has reared as a virtual brother to Ben but as a slave, nonetheless.

Comment

This book shows how the colonists fought bitter battles among themselves over land ownership. The authors describe the suffering of hard-pressed farm families who after years of building and working were summarily evicted by official decree or even by crafty speculators. People are pictured as tough and determined. Through Ben's eyes readers can sense the internal struggle of a young person questioning his father's seemingly paradoxical ideas of right and justice.

Suggestions for Reports or Activities

1. How did environmental issues contribute to the movement of settlers from eastern colonies into the wilderness?

2. Ben's father wanted to be free from his brother's domination, but yet he could not even consider Joe Mountain's desire for freedom. Discuss this apparent contradiction.

3. The struggle for survival in the wilderness made bitter enemies. Can you justify the actions of the Pennamites in trying to force the settlers from Connecticut to leave?

Burr, by Gore Vidal.
New York: Random House, 1975. 430p. (1)

Told in the form of two memoirs, one by Aaron Burr himself and the other by an imaginary young journalist whom Burr befriends in his old age, this novel recreates the significant historical period of the founding of this nation. Burr (1756-1836) was a hero of the American Revolution and vice-president under Jefferson. He also killed Alexander Hamilton in a duel and was tried for treason when Thomas Jefferson accused him of plotting to sever the western territories from the rest of the Union. Burr is an enigmatic figure. In this tale Gore Vidal affords him a fictional opportunity to present his own explanations of the apparent contradictions in his behavior.

Comment

Washington, Jefferson, Adams, Monroe, Madison, Hamilton, and others of the "founding fathers" are seen here through the eyes of a contemporary who did not think especially well of most of them. Students who know this period of history only through the conventional wisdom of their textbooks may be astonished to read of the foibles and failures of our early heroes. They should also be stimulated to further explorations of the character of Burr himself, a man of many weaknesses as well as strengths.

Suggestions for Reports or Activities

1. After comparing this account of Aaron Burr with others you have read, what is your opinion of Burr? Was he hero or traitor or fool? Support your conclusion with evidence from your readings.

2. What motivated James Wilkinson, governor of New Orleans? Is there any evidence that he was actually in the pay of Spain? What became of him?

Drums, by James Boyd.
New York: Scribner, 1925. 409p. (2)

Johnny Fraser, teenaged son of a Scottish farmer, lives a relatively simple country existence in the interior of North Carolina until he is sent east to a coastal town for his education. Not long after, war with England seems suddenly and surprisingly likely, when the English king refuses even to consider a Declaration of Rights from the First Continental Congress asking that he overrule Parliament's taxation decrees. Johnny is nonetheless sent to London on family business, to give him time to decide what to do. Ultimately, he chooses to side with the rebels and takes part in an exciting sea battle directed by the famous captain John Paul Jones.

Comment

Boyd presents a leisurely, detailed picture of life in the colonies at the time of the Revolution. His characters include Tories as well as rebels, townsfolk as well as country dwellers, women as well as men. The choices and conflicts faced by families of the time are depicted with some immediacy; thus Johnny's mother's family is loyal to the king, while his father's is not, a circumstance which encourages the boy to delay his decision to enlist. In the end circumstances permit no one to remain on the sidelines.

Suggestions for Reports or Activities

1. Locate some biographical information about John Paul Jones. Is there any evidence of his having acquired his name in the way described in this book? Did the battle of the *Bonhomme Richard* happen as Boyd said?

2. One of the loyalist characters in the book is a "collector" name Captain Tennant. What is a collector? What happened to collectors in other colonies—Massachusetts, for instance? Did they deserve this?

3. Think about Boyd's characterizations of blacks in this book. Why might we find these objectionable today? What is missing from these portraits?

The Fighting Ground, by Avi.
New York: Lippincott, 1984. 157p. (3)

In twenty-four hours spanning two April days, thirteen-year-old Jonathan changes his mind about war. He has been so anxious to fight. His father has returned home with a wounded leg. His older brother is a soldier; why not he? Early in the morning the bell tolls, and Jonathan goes to find out the news. A corporal says that some of the enemy are nearby. Jonathan admits that he knows how to fire a gun, and so he joins the little group of men. No one seems to know what the war is all about. Suddenly they confront several Hessian troops, and a skirmish takes place. Jonathan's interest in fighting begins to wane at the sight of blood; but now he is committed.

Comment

This short but quickly moving story points out to young readers that there is nothing pleasant about war. In his brief experience as a "soldier," Jonathan learns important lessons. The Hessians were enemies, but they could still be kind and gentle. The corporal whom he revered as a leader was also capable of viciousness. And his father was above all concerned for Jonathan's welfare.

Suggestions for Reports or Activities

1. You have probably read about the Hessian soldiers in your history text. What information does this story give you about the Hessians? Can you list some adjectives used to describe the Hessians in the story?

2. What were some of the events during that twenty-four-hour period that led Jonathan to change his mind about wanting to be a soldier?

3. Why did Jonathan break up the tavernkeeper's gun?

4. Jonathan's older brother is away fighting in the war. Write a letter that Jonathan might have written to his brother, telling about his experiences that day, and how he now feels about being a soldier.

Freelon Starbird, by Richard E. Snow.
Boston: Houghton Mifflin, 1976. 209p. (2, 3)

Freelon Starbird is an accidental soldier in the American Revolution. He has read Thomas Paine's tract *Common Sense* and has listened to his friend

Jib's bold statements about signing up, but he has also heard his father and uncle's protestation—why get involved in a foolhardy and doomed enterprise? But on the night celebrating the Declaration of Independence, an overindulgence in brandy leads Freelon to put his signature on a roll of recruits. His company of inexperienced young fellows drills, learns how to use their borrowed or makeshift firearms, and finally marches off, soon finding out that they do not know much about fighting. Alternatively brave or terrified, advancing or retreating, always ill-clad, hungry, cold, and often confused, the ragtag group crosses the Delaware to join George Washington.

Comment

The American Revolution may have been experienced by most of the unwitting recruits to the Continental army in this way—caught up in the excitement of the moment, not sure what the fighting was about, and unprepared. Readers will feel the uncertainties over enlisting, the occasional triumph, the urge to desert, and the harshness of winter (as formidable an enemy as the British). The author excels in evoking the feelings of personal and bodily stress on the field of battle.

Suggestions for Reports or Activities

1. Freelon is impressed by Thomas Paine's arguments in his book *Common Sense*. Read the book and paraphrase Paine's points. According to your text and other sources, what was the effect of Paine's writing on the colonists' feelings about the war?

2. In the beginning of the book Freelon complains about the common view expressed after the war, that the American Revolution was destined to be successful. John Adams wrote that the war was "only an effect and a consequence of it [the Revolution]. The Revolution was in the minds of the people, and this was effected . . . before a drop of blood was drawn at Lexington." If this is true, why was the war necessary?

The Hessian, by Howard Fast.
New York: Morrow, 1972. 192p. (2, 3)

A chain of events—a twist of circumstances—ends in apparently unavoidable tragedy. A squadron of Hessian soldiers—sixteen men and a drummer boy—are joined on their march by a dim-witted villager, carrying his slate and chalk. A spy? The Hessians think so and hang the man. Outraged, the townsfolk plan revenge and ambush the group, killing all but one. Hans Pohl, the sixteen-year-old drummer boy, is wounded, but he escapes and finds a hiding place at the farm of a Quaker family, the Heathers. Sally Heather, their teenage daughter, nurses Hans back to health, and the two fall in love. At length his whereabouts are discovered, and a trial is held.

Comment

This book calls attention to the role of the Hessian mercenaries in the American Revolution. The accidental nature of so much of the tragedy of war and the inevitability of unfairness are highlighted. The disdain with which the Quakers and Roman Catholics were regarded is evident. The starkness of the military trial, with its unyielding adherence to principle, is in harsh contrast to the tenets of Christian love expressed by the Quakers and Dr. Feversham.

Suggestions for Reports or Activities

1. Who were the Hessians? Where did they come from? What was their role in the American Revolution? Can you uncover any information on whether some of the Hessians remained in America after the war?

2. Can you imagine a way in which Hans' life could have been saved? Write another concluding chapter for this story.

3. Most readers identify with Hans and feel that he was wrongfully hanged, and this is what the author intends. What is the argument advanced by Squire Hunt? Write a short paper in which you justify his position.

I'm Deborah Sampson: A Soldier of the American Revolution, by Patricia Clapp.

New York: Lothrop, Lee & Shepard, 1977. 176p. (3)

Since her mother cannot afford to keep her, Deborah Sampson is "bound" at the age of ten to a good family with several sons. Deborah learns to run, plant, chop wood, and shoot as well as any boy her age. As she grows up, she falls in love with Robbie, one of the sons. Their romance is ended when Robbie goes off to fight for the Rebels and is killed. Wishing to "do something for Robbie," Deborah tucks her hair under her hat and enlists in the Continental Army. The often amusing adventures of a woman serving in a man's army add a lighthearted flavor to the sometimes grim accounts of the hardships of war.

Comment

Readers will feel involved in events leading to the war: taxes and restrictive laws enforced by the British. Specific events are mentioned, including the Boston Tea Party, Boston Massacre, the battles of Lexington and Concord, and the formation of the Continental Congress. Some important figures appear. The book conveys a sense of people uniting for a common cause as well as giving a feeling for the ordinary life of farmers during the 1770s.

Suggestions for Reports or Activities

1. Deborah Sampson was a real person. Can you find out about her in an encyclopedia or other source? What can you find out about her life after

the war ended? Does the account agree with the information in Clapp's book?

2. Deborah was a rather unusual young woman for her time. What can you discover about the role of women during the American Revolution?

3. The book describes some of the hardships suffered by soldiers during the Revolutionary War. Check in your textbook and in some reference sources to find out about day-to-day life in the Continental army.

John Treegate's Musket, by Leonard Wibberley.
New York: Farrar, Straus & Cudahy, 1959. 188p. (3)

John Treegate's musket had seen proud service on the side of England in the French and Indian Wars. And now, years later, with colonists' discontent mounting and talk of revolution in the air, Treegate remains fiercely loyal and vows that his musket will never be fired against the king. He sets off to England on business, leaving his son Peter presumably safely apprenticed to a barrel-stave maker in Boston. But shortly after, Peter finds himself accused of a murder and escapes aboard a merchant vessel bound for the French Indies. Shipwrecked off the coast of the Carolinas and suffering from amnesia, he is rescued and cared for by a Scottish hermit. Four years later, with his memory restored, he returns to Boston, to his father's great joy. But father and son soon find themselves on opposite sides in the growing revolutionary ferment. However, events cause the intractable John Treegate to change his mind. Joining with Peter, he shoulders his beloved musket and stands with the Patriots at the Battle of Bunker Hill.

Comment

Readers will sense the conflict of loyalties within a family and the build-up of tension in Boston. Peter's experiences aboard the *Maid of Malden* shed light on the colonists' efforts to find trade outlets and circumvent the restrictions imposed by the British. The poverty of the people of Boston during the British blockade is described. Important events such as the Boston Massacre, the Boston Tea Party, and the early battles of the war are part of the story.

Suggestions for Reports or Activities

1. What might have been some reasons for John Treegate's loyalty to England? Why might it have been easier for Peter to side with the Patriots?

2. Check in a reference source for more information on the plight of Boston merchants during the British blockade. Is the story of the *Maid of Malden* plausible?

3. What events led John Treegate finally to change his mind about his musket?

4. Who was Sam Adams? What was his role in the buildup of sentiment toward revolution?

Johnny Tremain, by Esther Forbes.
Boston: Houghton Mifflin, 1943. 238p. (1, 2, 3)

Silversmith apprentice Johnny Tremain is becoming skilled at his craft; his future is assured. He will marry one of his master's daughters and acquire half of the business. But an accident with hot, molten silver severely damages his hand. With no prospects for a livelihood, the desperate Johnny is befriended by Rab, a printer's helper. Rab aids him in getting a job delivering the *Boston Observer*, a publication of the Sons of Liberty, the Patriot leaders who are protesting England's treatment of the colonies. Johnny finds a role in the developing struggle. He is proud to join in the protest with the Sons of Liberty, and helps dump the tea in Boston Harbor. After the Battle of Lexington, when Rab is killed, Johnny learns that his hand is not hopelessly disabled and that he may be able to return to his trade. For now, most importantly, he can use it to fire Rab's musket in the Patriots' cause.

Comment

This story is both a look into the everyday life of the upper classes, the merchants and artisans, and the lowly apprentices of colonial Boston. It is an exciting picture of the city in ferment just before and in the early days of the Revolution. Samuel Adams, Paul Revere, Dr. Warren, and other figures in our history emerge as real people, and even British soldiers are human. The Boston Tea Party and the battles of Lexington and Concord are portrayed from the viewpoints of ordinary people involved in the events.

Suggestions for Reports or Activities

1. Johnny had hoped to become a silversmith. What other trades were possible careers for young people in Boston at the time? If you had been a young boy then, which of these might you have selected? What would you need to do to learn your craft?

2. It seems that not much was expected of young girls besides becoming proficient in household tasks. Is this true? What you can find out about the part played by women in Revolutionary Boston?

3. We don't read much about Paul Revere aside from his famous ride in Longfellow's poem. What can you find out about his role in history? (You might select one of the other members of the Sons of Liberty to investigate.)

Jump Ship to Freedom, by James Lincoln Collier
and Christopher Collier.
New York: Delacorte, 1981. 198p. (3)

Part two of the Arabus Family Saga, this book focuses on Daniel, a slave belonging to Captain Ivers. Daniel and his mother plan to buy their freedom with the soldier's pay notes from the American Revolution earned by Daniel's father. The father, however, dies on a sea voyage, and Mrs. Ivers takes the notes away from Daniel's mother. Daniel manages to steal back the notes, but Captain Ivers forces him onto a ship bound for the West Indies, where he will be expected to work in the cane fields. Daniel now must find a hiding place for the notes. When the ship docks in New York because of a storm, Daniel escapes to Sam Fraunces' tavern. From there he plots to retrieve the notes in order to buy his and his mother's freedom.

Comment

Daniel's misadventures involve the reader in the debate and compromise in the Constitutional Convention over the issue of slavery. The pay notes also play an important role, as Daniel deals with famous historical personages over the question of whether the individual states or the government to be formed by the convention should be responsible for paying them off.

Suggestions for Reports or Activities

1. Why was Daniel so upset about being a slave in the cane fields in the West Indies? Research the conditions in which slaves lived and worked there in this time period.

2. Read about the Constitutional Convention's quandary regarding slavery. What was the Connecticut Compromise? Write a short speech in which you try to convince the members of the Convention to abolish slavery altogether in the new nation.

3. Imagine that you are Daniel. Write an epitaph for Birdsey.

My Brother Sam Is Dead, by James Lincoln Collier and Christopher Collier.
New York: Four Winds, 1974. 216p. (3)

Tim Meeker tells the story of his family as it becomes involved in the American Revolution. Each family member has a different role and viewpoint. Tim's brother Sam, for instance, leaves his studies at Yale to become a "rebel" soldier. His father objects to all war and wishes to have no part of it. Tim's mother worries about her family's involvement in the Revolution, while Tim's own views change as he witnesses war's death and destruction. After his father disappears, the news of Sam's death and the problems of daily survival serve to confuse the remaining family members further as they seek to determine their ultimate loyalties.

Comment

The Meeker family's uncertainties mirror those of the conflict through which the United States was born. The authors contrast the views of the "rebels" revolting against oppression with those of the Loyalists fighting for their king and country. Both sides are portrayed as human; both sides make mistakes that cost lives. The book makes the young reader understand that there are many versions of what is right.

Suggestions for Reports or Activities

1. Many of the people and events mentioned here were real, as were all of the places. There even was a Meeker family in Redding. Select a person or event and research the historical accuracy of the version given here.

2. As the Meeker family is torn apart by opposing views, Tim realizes that there are more than two sides to the question. Write several pages from a journal Tim might have written as his loyalties changed.

3. Sam never loses his idealism, even when learning about the hardships of war. Imagine that you are Sam and write letters to Betsy Read describing your feelings about being a part of the American Revolution.

Oliver Wiswell, by Kenneth Roberts.
Garden City, N.Y.: Doubleday, 1952. 836p. (1, 2)

Oliver Wiswell—young, idealistic, educated, loyal to his government, son of a famous lawyer—finds himself exiled from his Boston area home by Rebel farmers and workingmen. These include his longtime neighbors the Leightons, the family of his sweetheart Sally. Oliver's travels and travails during the eight years covered by this tale take him from Boston to New York, London, Paris, the southern wilderness, a decisive battle not far from Charleston, and finally a new home in Nova Scotia at war's end. During all this time he and Sally manage to keep their faith in each other.

Comment

Told entirely from the point of view of the American Loyalists, this story makes a strong case for viewing the conflict as a civil war pitting friend against friend, brother against sister, child against parent. Most of the blame for losing the war is placed on the incompetent English generals who missed many chances to consolidate their early victories and thereby retain control of the colonies. Readers will be intrigued and challenged by this unfamiliar interpretation of our battle for independence.

Suggestions for Reports or Activities

1. Roberts describes the conditions which the members of Burgoyne's Convention army endured as prisoners of war, but he does not follow their

fates to the end of the war and beyond. Find out what happened, e.g., did any survive?

2. The British generals—Howe, Cornwallis, Clinton—come off badly in this story. Is there another view of their competence? Is it convincing?

3. How do you think Oliver's sweetheart Sally Leighton got along with the Loyalists in New Brunswick? Write a letter home from Sally to her mother, or a journal entry where she tells her secret and most honest reactions.

Rabble in Arms, by Kenneth Roberts.
New York: Doubleday, 1933. 586p. (1, 2)

As scouts for the American general Benedict Arnold, sea captain Peter Merrill and his brother Nathaniel take part in the campaigns of the Northern army, culminating in the battle of Saratoga which leads to General Burgoyne's defeat and capture. As a result, the British have to give up their plan to cut off New England from the rest of the colonies. The Merrills and their companions have many adventures, including being adopted into a tribe of Indians from the West and trying to outfox a woman spy who is spreading false rumors about General Arnold and the level of support for the Rebel cause.

Comment

Basing the title of his book on a quotation from General Burgoyne himself ("A rabble in arms, flushed with success and insolence"), Roberts stresses the contrast between the British regulars and the American woodsmen, farmers, sailors, and craftsmen who were fighting for their land and the right to determine their own destiny. General Arnold is defended throughout as a brave leader, a man of foresight and integrity who may have turned to the British in the end as a lesser evil than the French, toward whom the Congress appeared to be leaning.

Suggestions for Reports or Activities

1. A number of American generals—Schuyler, Gates, St. Clair, Sullivan—are mentioned here. Find out what sort of military careers they had after 1777 and the events narrated in this book.

2. Read an historical account of the battle of Saratoga where Burgoyne's forces were defeated. How is Arnold's role described?

3. What do you think motivated Marie de Sabrevois to betray her country? Write a letter from Marie to Ellen Phipps wherein she justifies her conduct.

Ruffles and Drums, by Betty Cavanna.
New York: Morrow, 1975. 222p. (3)

Sarah Devotion Kent witnesses the start of the American Revolution at the battle in Concord, Massachusetts. Sarah is sixteen, patriotic without reservation, and filled with longing to be a part of the action. She even becomes engaged to her childhood friend Tom because he is going off to war. After Sarah's father and brother join the rest of the neighbors to fight the British, reality sets it. Sarah and her mother must nurse a wounded British officer; life on the farm turns harsh without the help of the men; and to Sarah's consternation, she begins to change her unfavorable opinion of James, the British officer.

Comment

The American Revolution is depicted here through the feelings and reactions of a young girl. Readers will share the initial excitement of a country fighting for a cause, followed by the unromantic drudgery of daily life involved in running a farm, winding cartridge papers for the soldiers, and coping with shortages of food and clothing. Although Sarah still believes in freedom, as she matures she realizes that the reality of revolution is much less glamorous than the idea of it.

Suggestions for Reports or Activities

1. Research the origin of the American flag. What did the first flag look like? Draw a picture of the flag that Sarah would have seen in the 1770s.

2. Imagine that you are Sarah. Write several letters to a friend in which you describe your feelings about the war, Tom, and James.

3. Do further reading and research about the beginning of the American Revolution. Is the book accurate in its historical details? Make a chart with two columns. In the first column list the historical facts presented in the book. In the second column add new facts that you found in your research.

Sarah Bishop, by Scott O'Dell.
Boston: Houghton Mifflin, 1980. 230p. (2, 3)

Sarah Bishop's father is outspoken in his loyalty to King George. He dies after renegade rebels set fire to his house and barn, and torture him with tar and feathers. Sarah tries to locate her brother Chad, who has signed up to fight on the Patriots' side, but after weeks of searching she finds that he too has died. Wrongfully accused by the British of setting a major fire and threatened by a ne'er-do-well fellow who had offered her a ride, she flees to the wilderness, where through bitterness, stubborness, and inventiveness she makes her home in a cave. Living with a beaver and a bat for company, but cheered by the occasional visit of an Indian family, Sarah shuns people, seeking aid only when she needs to earn money for supplies. After being declared innocent of a charge of witchcraft, she does appear tentatively to reach out again to human society.

Comment

Ordinary people became innocent victims during the American Revolution. Being on the wrong side—or causing any suspicion—could result in being vandalized or murdered by one's neighbors. The war is depicted as both a civil war between Americans of opposing viewpoints and a war against English injustice. Sarah is shown as an example of the fortitude and independence of which colonial women were capable.

Suggestions for Reports or Activities

1. Different types of people are considered weird or peculiar in different periods of history. Do you think that Sarah Bishop would be considered an unusual person today? Would you like to have her for a friend? Explain.

2. We sometimes have been given the impression in our history books that the Patriots were the "good guys" and the Loyalists, or Tories, were the "bad guys." What have you found out in this book that either supports or contradicts this idea?

3. Textbooks often portray the Revolutionary War strictly as a fight between the Americans and the British. How does this narrative alter this picture?

1787, by Joan Anderson.
San Diego: Harcourt Brace Jovanovich, 1987. 200p. (2, 3)

The summer of the Constitutional Convention in Philadelphia is brought to life through the eyes of Jared Mifflin, Princeton student, assigned as an aide to James Madison. Jared's job is to facilitate the smooth running of the proceedings by taking care of details such as sufficient candles, controlling traffic in the State House area, and keeping the press away. It is quite a summer. Jared, who is from an upper-class family, makes two new friends: William, a servant of Benjamin Franklin, and Henry, the slave of a delegate from Georgia. Because of them he finds himself concerned about the new Constitution's provisions for the common man and for slaves. The most pleasing development of this most exciting summer is his growing fondness for Hetty Morris, an affection which she returns.

Comment

Against the backdrop of the love story of Jared and Hetty, the author has woven the story of the Convention, introducing the major actors and discussing the highlights and the major areas of debate, such as how to satisfy small and large states' concerns for adequate representation. Washington, Madison, Hamilton, Franklin, and others are shown in debate or at leisure. The life of the city is also described, as Jared moves from the State House to the docks, to a slave auction, to the market, to a fox hunt, and to a grand ball. The Constitutional Convention comes to life as a vibrant event.

Suggestions for Reports or Activities

1. After coming to know Henry and William, Jared found himself more concerned that the Constitution protect the rights of all citizens. What were the provisions of the Constitution regarding slavery? How was the Constitution amended to provide for individual rights?

2. What was the role of James Madison in framing the Constitution?

3. Why did the members of the Convention feel that it was necessary to keep the proceedings secret? Take both sides of the debate—the position of Weaver, the newspaper editor, and of James Madison—and list arguments for and against this policy.

4. Select a state and imagine that you are one of the delegates. Write a letter home to your constituents after the momentous signing of the Constitution.

Time Enough for Drums, by Ann Rinaldi.
New York: Holiday House, 1986. 249p. (2)

Jemima Emerson, high spirited and opinionated, is impatient with her strict and demanding tutor, John Reid, who appears to be a Tory spy. By the time she finds out he is working for the Americans, Jemima knows that he is in love with her, and the sentiment is mutual. The war is reaching close to home; Jemima discovers that her mother, unbeknownst to her father, is the secret author of letters to the newspapers seeking support for the Continental army; her brother Daniel enlists. Then the British occupy Trenton, her father is killed, and her mother appears to descend into an incurable depression. This story tells of one family's efforts to continue their lives in spite of the hardship and heartache of the war.

Comment

Through the everyday life in a quite prosperous family during the time of the battle of Trenton, the story shows how opinions differed over the rebels' (Patriots') cause. The British troops occupying the town are portrayed as reasonable, but the Hessians are stereotyped as uncouth ruffians. The somewhat contrived love story will not interfere with readers' gaining some understanding of the vicissitudes of war and its effects on ordinary people.

Suggestions for Reports or Activities

1. Jemima's mother had an unusual job for a woman for those times. What was the role of women during the American Revolution? Can you discover information about the activities of any specific woman or women of the period?

2. What famous work was written to arouse enthusiasm for the revolution? Research the role of the press in creating needed support among the rebels (or Patriots).

3. There is a famous painting called *Washington Crossing the Delaware*. Try to find a reproduction of this painting, and write a short paper describing what might have been the feelings of the men in the picture.

4. What was the importance of the battle of Trenton for the outcome of the war?

The Tree of Liberty, by Elizabeth Page.
New York: Literary Guild, 1939. 973p. (1, 2)

When James Howard dies in the course of General Braddock's defeat near the Forks of the Ohio, his son Matt, still in his teens, takes over responsibility for the family. Matt's lifetime parallels that of the beginnings of our country, stretching from the period just before the American Revolution through the return of the Lewis and Clark expedition from the Pacific Northwest. By 1806, Matt and his wife Jane are once again on the frontier, this time in Indiana with their own great-grandson, "Little Matt." Living through the Constitutional Convention and the presidential administrations of Washington, Adams, and Jefferson, they have learned much about democratic processes and politics along the way.

Comment

Differences of opinion among our early leaders are reflected by the major characters in this novel. When Matt's son Peyton suffers because of a prejudiced judge's interpretation of the Alien and Sedition Acts, when Peyton and his brother James take opposing sides in the conflicts between the Federalist Hamilton and the Democratic-Republican Jefferson, and when the revolution in France divides the family further—then aspects of our complicated political heritage are clarified in ways still meaningful today.

Suggestions for Reports or Activities

1. Research the election of 1800 between Adams and Jefferson. What laws were passed subsequently to prevent this kind of deadlock from recurring?

2. Early in the book class and sectional differences among the colonists are evident. What happens to make these less important as time goes on?

3. Invent a dialogue between Fleetwood Peyton and the first James Howard. Suppose they had lived to see their descendants: What would they think of them and the world in which they lived? Be specific in your comments.

War Comes to Willie Freeman, by James Lincoln Collier
and Christopher Collier.
New York: Delacorte, 1983. 178p. (3)

Willie Freeman is a thirteen-year-old free black girl. Her father was granted his freedom when he enlisted in the militia to fight the British. After witnessing her father's death in the battle of Fort Griswold (Connecticut), Willie learns that the British have taken her mother as a prisoner. Pretending to be a boy, Willie sets off on a journey to New York hoping to find her mother. This trip is especially dangerous because she is black; she has to avoid not only the war around her but also the possibility of being seized as a runaway slave. The story tells of Willie's adventures in New York, still posing as a boy. She finds some help at Sam Fraunces' Tavern in New York and later plays a role in a landmark New Haven court case that guarantees the freedom of Connecticut former slaves who fought in the Revolution.

Comment

The American Revolution is seen here through the eyes of a strong, intelligent girl who personally experiences the hardships of war and sees its effects on the people around her. The story recalls an actual incident, the famous court case *Arabus vs. Ivers.*

Suggestions for Reports or Activities

1. Blacks played a significant part in the American Revolution and the birth of this country. How is this important fact illustrated by this story? What additional information can you find in your text or other sources about blacks in the American Revolution.

2. What role did women play in society during this time period? Why did Willie have to pretend to be a boy? How did her friend Horace react when he discovered she was really a girl? How did his actions and attitudes change?

3. Draw a map of the British colonies in America during the Revolution. Trace Willie's journeys on the map. Be sure to include Fort Griswold and the various important places she visited on the way to New York.

Who Is Carrie?, by James Lincoln Collier and Christopher Collier.
New York: Delacorte, 1984. 158p. (3)

Part three of the Arabus Family Saga, this story centers around a kitchen slave named Carrie. A curious young person, Carrie is always getting into mischief, partly because of her inquisitiveness about her unknown personal history. She works in Sam Fraunces' famous tavern, which enables her to become part of the history of the post-revolutionary era. For example, when she is pursued by Captain Ivers, who wants to prove she is his slave, she hides by working in President George Washington's kitchen. Eventually, Carrie pieces together a plausible account of her own background.

Comment

Carrie becomes involved in various historical events. She witnesses Washington's inauguration and eavesdrops on conversations held by Thomas Jefferson and Alexander Hamilton. These experiences permit the modern reader a glimpse of our forefathers through the eyes of an ordinary young person, living at that time, before history had judged them great.

Suggestions for Reports or Activities

1. Write an advertisement for the lost-and-found section of the newspaper calling for additional background information on Carrie. Be sure to include the important known clues about Carrie's identity.

2. Write a letter from Carrie to Willie in which Carrie tells Willie about their possible relationship. Remember to include the tone of excitement that Carrie feels when she learns who she may be.

3. Find out more about the period when the nation's capital was located in New York City. Why was New York chosen? What problems did the choice create? Why was the seat of government moved? Where did it go, and when?

The Winter Hero, by James Lincoln Collier and Christopher Collier. New York: Macmillan, 1978. 152p. (3)

Justin looks up to Peter, his sister's husband, because he was a hero in the Revolution, and Justin would like to be a hero, too. But Peter is ready to fight again. Like other farmers in the area he is heavily in debt. They cannot pay the high taxes levied by the General Court, and the sheriff takes their plows, horses, or oxen. Peter is enraged when his oxen are seized and held by Mattoon, a wealthy landowner who has loaned him money. He decides to join in Captain Daniel Shays' scheme to protect the farmers' property rights. Peter gets Justin a houseboy's job at the house of Mattoon, supposedly to earn back the oxen but actually to be able to spy for Shays' "Regulators." Justin has several chances to show his bravery, to fight, and even to save Peter's life, twice. But he learns that being a hero is not without cost.

Comment

Shays' rebellion was the organized effort of citizens of several Massachusetts towns to shut down the courts to prevent the hearing of foreclosure cases. The authors have expanded on this incident to show an example of the growing pains of the new nation. Justin sees at first only the excitement of being allowed to join in a man's job but discovers that even a small war brings hurt and pain.

Suggestions for Reports or Activities

1. Read about Shays' Rebellion in your textbook or another source. What were the results? Would you say that it was a successful revolt?

2. Mattoon thought he had a right to take the farmers' oxen and plows. What was his argument? Do you think that he had any right to his position?

3. Why were the people of Pelham and the other towns upset with the General Court? Why couldn't they have any influence on the court?

III
THE CIVIL WAR
AND RECONSTRUCTION

Across Five Aprils, by Irene Hunt.
Chicago: Follett, 1964. 223p. (3)

Jethro learns early that the seeming glamor and thrill of war turn to pain as war comes close to home. His favorite brother, deploring slavery but detesting even more what many saw as Northern exploitation of the South, joins the Confederates. Despite the fact that two other brothers are fighting on the Union side, local ne'er-do-wells burn the family barn and poison their well. Although Jethro is only a young adolescent, he inevitably becomes part of the conflict, taking over the major farming chores after his father's heart attack, confronting his brother Tom's death in battle, struggling with his own conscience as he conceals his cousin Eb who is wanted as a deserter, and bravely daring to write of his concerns to President Lincoln. The family reaches that fifth April scarred but strong.

Comment

Against a background including descriptions of some battle details and discussions of war strategy, and showing how good people could have opposing opinions, the author has woven a story of feelings. Jethro, his siblings, and parents emerge as real human beings, suffering under circumstances they cannot help. Readers will gain an understanding of the complexities in explaining the Civil War and of the powerlessness of ordinary people.

Suggestions for Reports or Activities

1. Jethro was, of course, too young to fight in the Civil War, but nonetheless he was significantly involved. Describe how the war affected Jethro and forced him to mature.

2. Why has the author chosen the title *Across Five Aprils*? Explain the significance of April to understanding the story.

3. The Civil War was well reported in the newspapers. Research one of the campaigns mentioned in the story by checking the *New York Times* (or another paper) for its account of the event.

4. In past times young men have been excited by the idea of war. But some hired substitutes to fight for them, and others felt impelled to desert. What information can you find about desertion or about hiring substitutes.

Andersonville, by MacKinlay Kantor.
New York: Crowell, 1955. 760p. (1, 2)

Within hearing and smelling distance of the Claffey farm near Anderson, Georgia, a stockade is constructed in 1863 on 26 acres of swampland. Intended to serve as a prison for up to 10,000 captured Yankee soldiers, Andersonville eventually houses more than 30,000 at one time. Sanitation is primitive, rations are short, and prisoners prey upon each other; it is hardly surprising that thousands die every month. The author relives the horror of the details of prison life with vignettes of individual Yankee soldiers and with references to the fortunes of the nearby Claffeys (who had lost three sons in the first years of the war) and their neighbors.

Comment

The story of Andersonville, as told by MacKinlay Kantor, is essentially a true one. The modern reader will be appalled not only by the terrible conditions at the camp but also by the lack of accountability. Efforts by both military personnel and civilians to appeal to higher authorities for an end to the horrors consistently meet with failure. The trial of the camp superintendent, Captain Henry Wirz, after the South has surrendered clearly does not touch those who were ultimately responsible for the situation.

Suggestions for Reports or Activities

1. Check your public library for any of the books listed in Kantor's bibliography. Read enough to see how the account of Andersonville compares with that in this book. Does Kantor seem to have exaggerated?

2. Find out what happened at Henry Wirz's trial. What were the charges? What was his defense? What was the outcome of the trial?

3. Pick one of the young men at Andersonville whose story you have read. Imagine that he returned home to his loved ones. Describe his homecoming. What did he say? How was he received? How did he adjust to civilian life?

The Autobiography of Miss Jane Pittman, by Ernest J. Gaines.
New York: Dial, 1971. 245p. (1)

This saga is so convincing that it has been mistaken for a true story. The indomitable Miss Jane Pittman was freed from slavery at the end of the Civil War and lived to take a stand during the civil rights protests of the 1960s. Starting out naive but determined, she becomes a powerful figure, living out her long years, stalwartly facing grief and trouble, always proud. Her husband, Joe Pittman, is killed demonstrating his manhood while attempting to break a horse; her "son" Ned is ordered killed by whites for his supposedly radical teachings at his school for young blacks; and young Jimmy, the leader, perhaps the "One" the people have been waiting for, is sacrificed on the altar of black liberty during the civil rights demonstrations of the 1960s. Miss Jane Pittman, age 108 years or so, joins in the protest at the water fountain, as Jimmy had requested.

Comment

The book portrays life in the South as experienced from a black point of view, from the turmoil following emancipation all the way up to the civil rights era of the 1960s. Miss Jane Pittman typifies generations of solid, long-suffering black women, the ordinary unsung heroines of a century of slow change.

Suggestions for Reports or Activities

1. What was the message in Ned's sermon at the river (p. 106-112)? Compare his ideas with those of Martin Luther King, Jr., as expressed many years later in his speech during the March on Washington in 1963.

2. What did Miss Jane Pittman mean when she said (p. 234), "Freedom here is able to make a little living and hear the white folks say you good"? How does this differ from what Jimmy believed freedom to be?

3. Write a paper on the civil rights demonstrations in the South. Why was the time ripe?

4. If possible, conduct an interview with someone who participated in a protest march or demonstration for civil rights in the 1960s. Plan your interview to include your interviewee's impressions of progress in civil rights since that time.

Brady, by Jean Fritz.
New York: Coward, 1960. 223p. (3)

Brady Minton gets himself in trouble by talking when he should be quiet. He falls out of favor with his father when he mentions suspicious activity around hermit Drover Hull's cabin. Talk is in the air about runaway slaves. What Brady gradually comes to realize is that his own father, a minister, is helping to run a station on the Underground Railroad. When his father preaches a forthright sermon condemning slavery as an evil, opposition mounts in the congregation. Threatening notes appear. One night the barn is burned, and Reverend Minton is injured. In a daring secret effort to transport a young escaped slave boy to safety, Brady shows that he can be trusted.

Comment

For younger readers this story is an exciting introduction to the turmoil resulting from proslavery and antislavery sentiments existing in small-town America in the years before the Civil War. Brady's mother is from Virginia, and her feelings are different from those of his father; his brother is an abolitionist. People could agree that slavery was wrong and disagree on how to eradicate it. There is reference to John Quincy Adams and his antislavery stand in Congress. The incident showing an example of the operation of the Underground Railroad is real drama. The book shows how young people can be caught up in the everyday events of history taking place around them.

Suggestions for Reports or Activities

1. This book is largely a story of the Underground Railroad. Read about the Underground Railroad in an encyclopedia. Write a short paper about it.

2. Who were the abolitionists? Why does Brady ask Matt if he is an abolitionist?

3. Why was Bill Williams upset by Mr. McKain's Fourth of July speech? How do you think Tar Adams felt about that speech?

4. In the beginning Brady says that he doesn't know how he feels about slavery. How does he come to have strong opinions on this subject?

Bring Home the Ghost, by K. Follis Cheatham.
New York: Harcourt, 1980. 288p. (1, 2)

When they return from fighting in the Seminole war to find their home destroyed in an Indian raid, Jason and Tolin continue to share their lives under new circumstances. Tolin (white son of a slaveholding family) and Jason (Tolin's personal slave since both were children) travel west to a new life on the frontier, to excitement and danger. They vainly hope that they will be outside the range of the slave hunters. Tolin often expresses his belief that he and Jason are partners and equals; but since he is anxious for their partnership to continue, he delays showing Jason the freedom papers which he has already signed. When Jason begins to understand what freedom really means, he knows he must strike out on his own.

Comment

This book offers a perspective on the relationships of blacks and whites in the pre-Civil War period. It points out the precariousness of life for free blacks who were subject to capture and sale. Antislavery activities are highlighted, including the operation of a station on the Underground Railroad. Considerable attention is given to the Creek Indians and their relationships with blacks. The difference between being treated as a free man and actually being free is discussed.

Suggestions for Reports or Activities

1. How would you describe Jason's friendship with Tolin? How did this relationship change after the destruction of the Cobb estate? After Jason found out that he was free?

2. The book refers to some specific journals engaged in antislavery activity. What were some of the important abolitionist journals? Write a short paper on antislavery newspapers. The *Freedom Journal* is mentioned in the book. Write a short paper on black newspapers before the Civil War.

3. Indians of different tribes play a role in this story. Checking a reference source, what can you find out about the Seminole war? About the relationships of Creek Indians and blacks?

The Chaneysville Incident, by David Bradley.
New York: Avon, 1981. 450p. (1)

John Washington, a historian, returns to the black section of the small Pennsylvania town where he grew up to see his dying guardian. The old man tells stories about John's father, Moses Washington, and his great-grandfather, C. K. Washington; these accounts fill in some details on the history of this black family. This recounting of stories out of the past becomes a saga of enraging experiences which blacks suffered under slavery and its aftermath. It reflects the strength and determination of blacks who remained still in touch with the natural environment and the African inheritance. John Washington's tools as a historian are used to piece together some unknowns. In the retelling of many stories, John works through the possibility of a positive interracial relationship for himself.

Comment

This book allows the reader to feel the deep resentments blacks felt as a consequence of the slavery system and how these resentments lingered on from generation to generation. The toughness and resourcefulness of the black resistance are well illustrated as are many of the weaknesses of whites, themselves victims of their own repression of others.

Suggestions for Reports or Activities

1. What is the significance of the two sides of the hill where the black community lived?

2. John Washington says repeatedly that history is "atrocious," i.e., a series of atrocities. What is the basis of this designation? Suggest another term to describe the meaning of the "stories" that are strung together in the book.

3. Describe the nature of the relationships between whites and blacks presented in the book.

Cowslip, by Betsy Haynes.
Nashville: Nelson, 1973. 139p. (3)

When thirteen-year-old Cowslip is sold to Colonel Sprague, her life begins to change. Mistress Sprague is going on a trip and Cowslip is needed to look after the children. Working in the Sprague house, she meets Job, one of the older slaves, who has an air of mystery. Hearing talk about freedom for the first time, Cowslip begins to realize that she too is a person with dignity. Job astonishes her when he says she should learn to read and write. Whispers about running away are in the air. Reba does try to get away, with her man Percy, but they are caught and shot as an example to the others. Cowslip is sure now: she's going to live up to her name and be like the flower, the cowslip, that blooms wild and free.

Comment

This book gives young readers some solid information about conditions under slavery. Through various actions the slaves cleverly tricked their white masters. Barbarously cruel treatment is portrayed (the auction block and the whip). Readers will learn that this was a time of great contradictions, as it became constantly more difficult to keep the system working.

Suggestions for Reports or Activities

1. Look up the Underground Railroad in an encyclopedia. How did it work? Where were some of the stations located? See if you can find a map which locates these "stations." Draw a copy of this map.

2. Who was Harriet Tubman? Write a short paper describing why she was important.

3. Cowslip is surprised to find out that she can learn to read and write. What were some of the means used by slaveholders to keep their slaves under control? What were some of the means used by the slaves to resist their oppressors?

Elkhorn Tavern, by Douglas C. Jones.
New York: Holt, 1980. 311p. (1, 2)

Martin Hasford has gone to fight for the Confederacy. His wife, Ora, and teenaged children, Roman and Calpurnia, are diligently struggling to keep up their Arkansas farm. The war comes closer than they expected. They must protect themselves against marauding "bushwackers" and "jaywalkers," armed men masking as soldiers who forage and loot while claiming to support one cause or the other. The little-known and bloody battle of Pea Ridge is fought in the hills around their farm. Ora is tough, a woman of high principles, and her children are imbued with her courage. When a wounded Yankee officer is brought to their doorstep Ora acts quickly to save him. During his slow recovery all of their lives change.

Comment

In this gripping story of courage and survival the strong woman is the true hero. Ora (and Calpurnia, too) exhibits the will to endure and the ability to make the right choices in extreme circumstances. Readers will experience the war from the point of view of people supposedly on the sidelines, but yet finding themselves in the crossfire. The ruggedness of farm life in the last century is graphically depicted, as is the suffering on the battlefield.

Suggestions for Reports or Activities

1. The book makes it clear that the Civil War involved more than generals and battles and that women who were left behind played an important role. Based on what you have learned about the war in this book, write a short paper on the war from Ora or Calpurnia's point of view.

2. Martin Hasford did not enlist to support the practice of slavery. Check your textbook and an encyclopedia for causes of the Civil War. Then in a short paper give reasons why Martin and many other southern men joined in the war effort.

3. There are numerous incidents that depict the character of Ora and of Calpurnia. Drawing on these incidents, write a short paper on either Calpurnia or Ora as examples of women who can succeed in spite of the problems they face.

Freedom Road, by Howard Fast.
New York: Duell, Sloan & Pearce, 1944. 263p. (3)

Gideon Jackson, former slave and former Union soldier, returns to South Carolina to find a new world opening for him and his children. At first shamed by his inability to read and write and his lack of experience with the sophisticated world of Charleston, Gideon moves painfully but bravely into his new roles, first as delegate to the Convention aiming to write a new constitution for the state and, much later, as a member of the House of Representatives of the Congress of the United States. When Northern troops are withdrawn from the South in 1877, attacks by the Ku Klux Klan put an end to a temporary idyll created by the willing cooperation of whites and blacks.

Comment

Young people today may imagine that it is only since the civil rights agitation of the 1960s that people of different colored skins have been able to live, study, and work together as friends. Fast's book makes it clear that such a situation indeed existed nearly a hundred years earlier, brought to a tragic end by northern inattention and a southern white desire to restore prewar power relationships insofar as possible.

Suggestions for Reports or Activities

1. Fast blames President Grant for much of what happened in the South after his successor, Rutherford B. Hayes, took office. What do you know about the Hayes-Tilden election and what happened afterwards? Could Grant have acted differently from the way he did? Explain your answer.

2. Compare the activities and philosophy of the Ku Klux Klan in the 1870s and 1880s with those of the Klan today. How are they different or alike?

3. The character of Gideon Jackson was based on those of several black congressional representatives of the time. Find out all you can about two or three of these first black legislators.

A Gathering of Days: A New England Girl's Journal, 1830–1832, by Joan Blos.
New York: Scribner, 1979. 144p. (3)

Catherine Hall, age thirteen, begins her journal of a year and a half on her family's New Hampshire farm. Her mother is dead; she and her sister Matty live with their father. Next door live Cassie Shipman, Catherine's best friend, and her brother Asa. Catherine writes of ordinary happenings—chores, school, church, and occasional celebrations. Some excitement is experienced when a "phantom" (a runaway slave) leaves a note in the woods and the children have to make some decisions on their own. Two significant personal events are recorded, the remarriage of her father to a woman with a son Catherine's age and the sudden death of Cassie. But life goes on, and a new adventure awaits Catherine as her journal ends.

Comment

The story depicts everyday life and annual events such as maple syrup gathering, spring planting and cleaning, berry picking and quilting. Thanksgiving and Fourth of July celebrations are described. Stories, jokes, verses, and recipes from the time help to bring the period to life. School life is vividly portrayed. The incident with the runaway slave shows how the major issue of the times, slavery, reached even this remote New England farmland.

Suggestions for Reports or Activities

1. Describe life on a New England farm in the 1830s.

2. What can you find out about the impact of slavery on the attitudes of New Englanders during the 1830s?

3. Catherine and her friends attended a one-room schoolhouse. How were these schools organized? What was life like for a teacher in such a school? Are there still one-room schoolhouses in the United States today?

4. For a group activity, plan an almanac for a year's farming in New England. Include phases of the moon, equinoxes, solstices, snowfalls, rainfalls, droughts. Include recommendations for planting, harvesting, syrup making, etc.

Gone with the Wind, by Margaret Mitchell.
New York: Macmillan, 1939. 1037p. (1)

The spoiled but charming Scarlett O'Hara is the heroine of this lengthy and engrossing novel, set in Georgia in and near Atlanta. Twice Scarlett marries men whom she does not love, all the while pining for Ashley Wilkes, the husband of her friend, Melanie. The dashing bachelor Rhett Butler drifts in and out of her life and eventually becomes her third husband. In the meantime, Scarlett sees her beloved plantation Tara burned and pillaged at the time of General Sherman's ''march to the sea.'' Forced at last to take care of herself and others, Scarlett finally grows up.

Comment

Familiar to many readers as a famous film, *Gone with the Wind* nevertheless paints as vivid a picture through words as the movie does through photographic images of a world destroyed by war. The impact of Sherman's march to Atlanta and the subsequent destruction of one of the South's most beautiful cities is shattering. Scarlett herself is too headstrong to evoke constant sympathy, but interest in her fate leads the reader to learn a lot about the period from the white southern aristocrat viewpoint.

Suggestions for Reports or Activities

1. Based on the novel, what roles did women play during the Civil War? Was Scarlett O'Hara typical or atypical? What traits enabled her to survive?

2. Sherman burned some of the South's major cities in the course of his march. Find out from historical sources if Mitchell's description of the burning of Atlanta is accurate; if it is not, speculate why not.

3. Investigate the roles taken by slaves during the Civil War. What places did they have in the armies of both sides?

4. Write a journal from the point of view of Melanie or one of Scarlett's sisters. How might they have viewed the war? Scarlett? Tara?

Hew against the Grain, by Betty Sue Cummings.
New York: Atheneum, 1977. 174p. (2)

In this book an adolescent girl is confronted with important, vital problems as her life revolves around the events of the Civil War. Mattilda realizes that her best friend Dorcia, who is a slave, is considered to be property. Although her Virginia family chooses not to believe in slavery, her brothers find themselves divided by their loyalties. Their conflict stems from disagreement not over slavery so much as the question of each state's right to self-government. As the war devastates the community, Mattilda becomes a source of strength and courage. Neighbors once considered harmless turn into enemies, even fanatics, who hate her, especially for her friendship with Dorcia. These feelings end only when Mattilda kills her rapist neighbor.

Comment

The brutality of war brings grief and self-examination to this family. Mattilda sees the destruction of her land and life as she has known it, as well as the defeat of spirit of the people around her. The war plays a powerful role in the lives of everyone, black and white, as their relationships with each other are changed forever. Here is a moving portrayal of a girl who becomes a woman of substance through necessity.

Suggestions for Reports or Activities

1. Examine the issue of states' rights from Mattilda's and Dorcia's points of view. How do they differ? Why do they differ?

2. How would living on the border of Virginia and West Virignia affect a person's attitudes during the Civil War? Write an editorial for a newspaper in a border town in favor of siding with either the North or the South.

3. How did the relationship of Mattilda and Dorcia change during the war? What common events happened to them? How did they become "equal" at last?

High Hearts, by Rita Mae Brown.
New York: Bantam, 1986. 424p. (1)

This is the story of eighteen-year-old Geneva Chatfield's adventures with the First Virginia Cavalry, which she joins in the guise of a man in order to be with her new husband Nash Hart. Geneva proves to be a better soldier than Nash, to their mutual discomfort. A range of attitudes toward the war is expressed by the other characters, both historical and fictional; among the latter are members of Geneva's family, the slaves on their plantation near Charlottesville, residents of Richmond, and other cavalrymen. It is only after much bloodshed and painful learning that the relationships among the characters are satisfactorily worked out.

Comment

The special focus of this novel is the sacrifices made by women and slaves on behalf of the Confederacy. One aristocratic woman, for example, finds her life changed irrevocably by the call to nurse the wounded Confederate soldiers. A young slave finds that she has to leave the only home she has ever known when she and a white soldier fall in love. Others react to the death and mutilation of their menfolk and the destruction of their way of life with courage or despair. The author makes especially graphic the primitive medical care and supplies available to the wounded and dying of both armies as they return to town by the trainload following each battle.

Suggestions for Reports or Activities

1. Read an historical account of the Battle of Manassas Junction (July 21, 1861). How does it compare with the version given here?

2. Geneva mentions that the slave Di-Peachy and Mercer did get married but were not happy. Write your own account of what might have happened to them.

3. Pick one of the historical characters (such as Stuart, Longstreet, Davis, McClellan, or Stephens) and find out what became of him after the war.

Jubilee, by Margaret Walker.
Boston: Houghton Mifflin, 1966. 497 p. (1)

The years of the Civil War period, before and after, are recounted from the imagined point of view of Vyry, a slave woman, who was the author's great-grandmother. Vyry's mother had been the favored slave mistress of the plantation owner, Marse Dutton, and at an early age Vyry comes to live in the big house, first as playmate and servant to Marse's daughter, and eventually as head cook. Wooed by a free black, she bears him two children, but his attempt to buy her is thwarted by her owners, and her effort to run away to join him ends in a merciless beating. Then comes the war and everything is turned upside down. Vyry surmounts the destruction and death that surround her and finds herself loved by a good man. Together they are able to begin building a life despite a series of harrowing events which were commonplace for blacks during the years after the war. Her dream of an education for her children begins to seem possible.

Comment

Reminiscent of *Gone with the Wind* for its sweep of history and its saga of the life of one woman, this book is rich in details of life in the Old South from the point of view of a person born and raised in slavery. It depicts relationships among people—between blacks, between whites, between blacks and whites—and shows the struggles for power and for equality that were part of southern society, particularly in the period after the war. Readers will realize that emancipation did not happen at once, and the difficulties in making freedom a reality. The story describes the horrors of the persecution of blacks both before and after the Civil War. Readers will gain a sense of the courage, resourcefulness, and resilience of people in dreadful circumstances.

Suggestions for Reports or Activities

1. What were the differences in policy between the moderate plan for reconstruction advocated by Lincoln and the methods of the Radical Republicans?

2. There are lines from Negro spirituals at the beginning of each chapter foreshadowing events in the chapter. Select three of these introductory fragments. In a reference work locate the rest of the words. How is the spiritual a clue to what is going to happen in the chapter?

Rifles for Watie, by Harold Keith.
New York: Crowell, 1957. 332p. (3)

Jeff Bussey knew he was doing the right thing when he left his family's Kansas farm to join the Union forces. The Union was fighting to ensure the freedom of all men; hence they had the best cause on their side. Besides, the war would not last long, and he would have a chance for glory. At least, that was what Jeff thought. Once enlisted, however, he discovers that being in the army is mostly dull routine drills. Then when he finally participates in a real battle, Jeff quickly discovers that war is not at all glorious. Eventually he is sent behind enemy lines as a spy. His perspective of war is further enlightened when he realizes that the men of the South share the same concerns for family and farm as he and his Union comrades.

Comment

The author's use of primary sources to research the setting results in a very convincing tale. The action is centered around the far western theater of the war. Readers will read about the conflict between Missouri and Kansas, the issue of states' rights, the gun trafficking between North and South, and the role played by the Cherokee nation. The hardships of life at the front and the involvement of civilians living near the scene of battle are vividly described.

Suggestions for Reports or Activities

1. Stand Watie was an actual person. Using a reference source, find out some information about his role in the Civil War. How accurate is the information in the novel?

2. In this book, various opinions are expressed by different characters on the most important issues in the war, and on why they are involved. (For example, Jeff wants to fight the bushwackers; Lucy Washbourne feels that the United States government has betrayed her people.) Compare and contrast two additional Union views with two additional Confederate views.

3. Assume that Jeff kept a journal of his war years. Write an entry as though you were Jeff describing a day when an important event took place.

4. Find out about the Cherokee nation and its role in the Civil War.

Roots: The Saga of an American Family, by Alex Haley.
Garden City, N.Y.: Doubleday, 1974. 688p. (1)

Drawing on the oral traditions handed down in his family for generations, Alex Haley traces his origins back to the seventeen-year-old Kunta Kinte who was abducted from his home in Gambia and transported as a slave to colonial America. It was Kinte's insistence on teaching African words to his daughter and describing his earlier life that initiated the sequence of repetitions that many generations later led the author to visit the village from which his ancestor had come. Later made into a television miniseries, this account provides an imaginative rendering of the lives of seven generations of black men and women in this country.

Comment

Since more than half of the book is devoted to a careful reconstruction of the "African's" life under slavery, it is especially valuable to the reader for insights into this period. Most of the rest of the book deals with the lives and fortunes of Kunta Kinte's grandson, Chicken George, and his family, with just the last hundred pages or so chronicling the remaining generations.

Suggestions for Reports or Activities

1. See what you can find out about Alex Haley. What else has he written? What has he done since the publication of *Roots*?

2. If you check the *New York Times Index* under the name Haley for the year 1976 or 1977, you should find mention of a controversy which began when another writer accused Haley of having plagiarized something he had written. Who was this other writer and what was the outcome of the controversy?

3. The slaves in this book always found out indirectly what was going on in the world. Name some of the ways in which they received such news and give examples of the impact on them of events occurring far away.

The Sacred Moon Tree, by Laura Jan Shore.
New York: Bradbury, 1986. 209p. (2, 3)

Phoebe Sands has a tendency to imagine, to jump to conclusions, and to fabricate (perhaps an inherited gift for blarney and seeing fairies and sacred moon trees), but she has no problem convincing others to go along with her impetuous, seemingly hairbrained schemes. Observing what she thinks are suspicious actions, she concludes that her Richmond-bred mother is a Confederate spy. Later her father, taunted by her mother from being a coward, joins the Union army, and her mother takes off to Richmond, presumably to care for her sick grandfather. Phoebe is determined to go to Richmond. Learning that her friend Joth's brother Nate is in a Confederate prison there, Phoebe dresses as a boy and masterminds a plan to get herself and Joth to Richmond to try to rescue Nate. Unexpected help makes the venture a success.

Comment

This informative and exciting adventure story depicts how the Civil War was experienced by two lively and inventive young people. The tensions between family members with opposing views on the war are dramatically conveyed. The children suffer hunger, witness fighting, and see the desperate plight of the wounded. The imagined glamor of war fades as danger, devastation, and death become real.

Suggestions for Reports or Activities

1. What was the importance of Richmond during the Civil War?
2. Can you find any information about the role of spies during the Civil War?
3. What is the significance of the title?

The Slave Dancer, by Paula Fox.
New York: Bradbury, 1973. 176p. (2, 3)

Jessie Bollier is kidnapped near the docks in New Orleans and forced aboard a ship heading for West Africa. He finds conditions aboard ship intolerable. The crew is a scurvy bunch, cruel to each other, led by a brutish captain. Food is bad, water is scarce, sleeping quarters are dark and cramped, and Jessie is miserable. When the ship arrives in Africa and takes on its human cargo, Jessie finds out why he is there: to play his fife in order to "dance the slaves." This is a method of providing some exercise so that slaves can be kept in somewhat better health for the marketplace. Jessie is degraded by this role and sickened by the lot of the blacks, quartered on top of each other in the stench-filled hold. Many become ill, die, and are thrown overboard. The ship withstands a challenge by a British antislavery vessel, but then it is wrecked in a fierce storm; almost everyone is lost.

Comment

This story depicts how the slave trade worked, the rationale of necessity and profit which made it seem legitimate, and how the trade continued long after Congress had outlawed it. Appalling conditions aboard ship are graphically described, both the inhuman nature of the sailors' lives (men who were scarcely more than slaves themselves) and the despicable treatment of the blacks on the voyage. The actions of the British fleet, both in attacking slave ships and in searching for deserting British sailors, are described. Jessie's reaction to his plight gives readers a view from a sensitive young person exposed to the horrors of such a voyage.

Suggestions for Reports or Activities

1. Find out about the British attitude toward the slave trade. What actions did the British navy take against slave ships? Does the account in the story seem plausible, based on what you have learned in other sources?

2. New Orleans was a bustling shipping center in the mid-nineteenth century. Read about the port of New Orleans. Write a report describing the commercial activities taking place there.

3. In the book Ras is helped to escape north to freedom. Invent a story of his journey.

The Slopes of War: A Novel of Gettysburg, by N. A. Perez.
Boston: Houghton Mifflin, 1984. 202p. (2,3)

The battle of Gettysburg is encountered from a number of viewpoints in this moving story. In the background are the deliberations and decisions of generals and officers from both armies, all portrayed as human beings grappling with destiny. Against this fact-based setting is woven the story of sixteen-year-old Bekah Summerhill and her family, who live in Gettysburg and are unwitting actors in the drama around the battle. Bekah's story includes that of her brother Buck, enlisted with a Pennsylvania regiment, and of Custis, her favorite cousin, fighting for the Confederacy. The three days in July changes all of their lives. President Lincoln's address several months later helps the events make sense to Buck.

Comment

What was happening at Gettysburg? The author describes the battle maneuvers and evokes the confusion felt by the generals, but brings the event dramatically to life through focusing on the experiences of young boy soldiers who are newly aware that there is little glamor in actual combat. Most vivid is the picture of how the townspeople, particularly Bekah—all merely interested bystanders at first—rise heroically to the fact of the battle around them; they provide food and clothing to stragglers from both sides, dodge flying shells, care for the wounded, and come to terms with death. The concluding chapter on Lincoln's visit to dedicate the cemetery provides a poignant comment on this episode in our history.

Suggestions for Reports or Activities

1. What actually happened at Gettysburg? Why was it such a pivotal event? Why was President Lincoln upset at the results?

2. Suppose that General Meade had followed through on Lincoln's orders. How might the course of the war gone? Check this in your textbook and in some reference sources.

3. How do you think that Bekah changed during the days of the battle? Discuss the effect of the war being fought on their doorstep on the lives of ordinary people in the town.

The Tamarack Tree: A Novel of the Siege of Vicksburg,
by Patricia Clapp.
New York: Lothrop, Lee & Shepard, 1986. 214p. (3)

Arriving from England to live with her brother in Vicksburg, Rosemary finds that she has a lot to get used to. Outraged by the idea of slavery, she finds it difficult to follow her brother's advice and keep her opinions to herself while trying to settle into her new community. But she soon grows to love the gracious life shared with her southern belle friend, Mary Byrd, the dancing parties, the charming young men. Then comes the war, the blockade, and the disappearance of accustomed luxuries and necessities. Now the worst has happened. The Union ships are bombarding Vicksburg. Life is changing for everyone and maybe, says Rosemary, for the better.

Comment

The author has portrayed the pride, the fear, and the determination of the people of Vicksburg as they tried to fortify their hills to repulse the Union advance. Conversations for and against slavery show how conflicting ideas tried friendships. The author shows how visitors from another country might have reacted to the institution of slavery. There is a description of the operation of one station on the Underground Railroad. The positive pictures of Amanda and Hector, and particularly of Hector's role in the struggle for freedom, provide an example of the role of the free black in Civil War society.

Suggestions for Reports or Activities

1. Rosemary and Jeff quarrel over the reasons for the conflict between North and South. Mary Byrd and Derek also have a bitter disagreement. Compare the points these characters make with the reasons given in your textbook or other source.

2. Locate Vicksburg on a map. Why was the city an important target for the Union army? Research the effect that the war had on shipping on the Mississippi River.

3. Amanda and Hector were free blacks living in the South during the Civil War. What can you find out about the life of free blacks at that time?

Tancy, by Belinda Hurmence.
New York: Clarion, 1984. 203p. (2)

Tancy's life as a house slave is suddenly changing. Master Gaither has just died; Miss Pudding is in charge now. With her son Billy forced to join the Confederate army, Miss Pudding depends so much on Tancy. But the war is almost over, and the slaves are free. What does that mean for Tancy? Her hope is to find her mother, sold away from Gaithers when Tancy was only a baby. At first Tancy hesitates to leave Miss Pudding with no one to count on, Billy dead now from the war, all the folks going off. But times are different now. Tancy is determined to find her own way. It's scary out there away from the plantation, but Tancy discovers she has strength and sense.

Comment

Told from the point of view of sixteen-year-old slave girl Tancy, this is a moving account of the plight and the resilience of blacks during the dying days of slavery and the upheaval following the Emancipation Proclamation. It is also the story of the plight of whites who had learned from birth their superiority and were ill-prepared to cope with the new age brought on by the South's collapse. Billy's thwarted attempts to rape Tancy before he is dragged off to war are symbolic. With background drawn from the collection of slave narratives at the Library of Congress, this account looks realistically at the chaos of the Freedmen's Bureau and the early attempts to provide education for newly freed blacks.

Suggestions for Reports or Activities

1. The Gaithers lived in an area of North Carolina that had been opposed to secession. Check in your textbook or a reference source for information on pockets of resistance to the Confederacy. What were some reasons for this resistance?

2. What was the purpose of the Freedmen's Bureau? Was it successful? Write a short paper describing its activities and results.

3. Write an outline for another chapter describing Tancy's life after the end of the book. Do you suppose she continued to work at the bank? Did she decide to become a teacher after all? Why?

This Strange New Feeling, by Julius Lester.
New York: Dial, 1982. 149p. (1, 2, 3)
    Three short stories adapted from slave narratives describe daring escapes. In the first, "This Strange New Feeling," Ras (who has run off once and has been brought back to the plantation) cleverly tricks his master and helps other slaves run away. As he and Sally attempt their own escape, Master blocks their path, but Sally moves quickly. In "Where the Sun Lives," Maria is about to be freed according to her husband's will, but his unpaid debts doom her hopes. "A Christmas Love Story" chronicles the brave adventure of William and Ellen Craft who plan an ingenious masquerade to win their freedom. A pallid young "man," obviously a frail invalid, accompanied by "his" man-servant, boards the train for Philadelphia. Freedom! But the passage of the Fugitive Slave Law makes their new life a nightmare.

Comment
    These stories by the author of *To Be a Slave* reveal the often forgotten ingenuity of the black slave in the United States. Readers will be reminded of how slaves often pretended to be dumb or foolish, and were skillful in say-ing what they knew their masters wanted to hear. The stories describe the feel-ings of blacks in bondage, the humiliation of the auction block, the cruel suffering of corporal punishment, the ability to accommodate, and the unflag-ging zeal for freedom. The activities of some of the Northern abolitionists and reaction to the Fugitive Slave Law are depicted.

Suggestions for Reports or Activities
    1. The third story mentions the Fugitive Slave Law signed by President Fillmore. Other fugitive slave laws were enacted earlier. What were the pro-visions of these laws? How did northern states respond to the 1850 law?
    2. Check in a biographical source for information about Thomas Par-ker. Who were some of the other well-known abolitionists? Write an account of the activities of another abolitionist.
    3. Research some other accounts of attempts by slaves to secure their freedom.
    4. The Underground Railroad had many conductors, black and white, and stations in many parts of the North. Write a short paper on the Under-ground Railroad in a specific part of the country. Include a map.

Three Days, by Paxton Davis.
New York: Atheneum, 1980. 102p. (1, 2, 3)

General Robert E. Lee is planning a decisive strike against the Union army forces when they are least expecting it, deep in Yankee territory. Through this maneuver he hopes to end the war with less destruction to the South. Therefore, he has the Army of Northern Virginia moving through Pennsylvania. But all the audacity and cunning of Lee and his generals cannot withstand General Meade and the strength and numbers of the Army of the Potomac. The story is well-known. This book recounts the events of the days of Gettysburg from Lee's anguished viewpoint. Along with Lee's story are the brief and poignant musings of a young Confederate soldier.

Comment

Three Days is a step-by-step account of Lee's failed strategy at Gettysburg and of the devotion of his generals. The picture of a great man suffering with his decision is moving. The wasteful carnage of the battle is graphically depicted in this three-day memoir.

Suggestions for Reports or Activities

1. Check in your textbook and in another source for information on Lee's plans for overcoming the Union army in northern territory. According to the novel, why did Lee fail? Does this account seem accurate, based on information in other sources?

2. Aside from Lee, several other important Confederate generals are mentioned in the book, including Stuart, Longstreet, Hill, Pickett, and Stonewall Jackson. In an encyclopedia or biographical source find information about the life of one of these men. (You may compare his background with that of General Lee.)

3. The author states, "History often hinges on trivia" (p. 17). To what is he referring? Is this a true incident? How might the battle of Gettysburg been different if this "trivial" incident had not occurred?

Turn Homeward, Hannalee, by Patricia Beatty.
New York: Morrow, 1984. 193p. (3)

Twelve-year-old Hannalee has promised her mother that she will find her way back home. Yankee soldiers from Sherman's army have descended upon her hometown of Roswell, Georgia, burned the mill, and rounded up all the mill hands, transporting them north to replace much needed workers in Kentucky and Indiana. Caught in this tumultuous scheme are Hannalee, her younger brother Jem, and Rosellen Sanders, who is her older brother's sweetheart. The three vow to stay together, but this plan soon is shown to be impossible. Hannalee decides to look for Rosellen; but when it is clear that

Rosellen is changing her mind about trying to return home, Hannalee knows she must depend on herself. She locates her brother Jem, disguises herself as a boy, and together, after some frightening adventures, they find their way back to Roswell.

Comment

Readers will learn of a little-known incident of the Civil War, the capturing of southern mill workers, and shipping them to northern factories, or to serve in northern homes. Using this actual happening as background, the author focuses on how the Civil War touched ordinary people. As she states in an author's note, too much of our impression of the war is based on stories of the aristocracy, such as *Gone with the Wind*. The senseless destruction of property as well as of human beings is movingly depicted through Hannalee's eyes. This spunky heroine shows the resilience of people in times of necessity.

Suggestions for Reports or Activities

1. Read the author's note on the mill workers. Then check into some reference sources to locate additional information on this topic.

2. Sherman's march through Georgia was an important part of the campaign in the South. Read about Sherman's activities in your textbook and in some other sources. Write a short paper on the outcome and effects of Sherman's march.

3. Hannalee states that her family never had slaves. Yet they were loyal southerners. Can you find information on what percentage of southern families were slaveholders? Write a short paper on this subject.

The 290, by Scott O'Dell.
Boston: Houghton Mifflin, 1976. 118p. (3)

The 290 chronicles the adventures of sixteen-year-old Jim Lynn from New Orleans who at the start of the Civil War is working as a shipbuilder's apprentice in Liverpool, England. During the war he signs on as a sailor on the *Alabama*, a ship he helped to build. Its mission is to seek out and destroy the Union navy. The story vividly describes the battles in which the *Alabama* engaged and recounts an attempted mutiny. It also describes Jim's efforts to free hundreds of slaves held prisoner in Haiti by his father and his father's partner, pending shipment to Cuba.

Comment

The *Alabama* was one of the most famous Confederate ships. The fact that it was built and fitted in England was considered by the United States government to be a violation of neutrality agreements. Because of heavy damage done to the Union navy by the *Alabama* and other British-built ships, claims were filed by the United States against Britain. The book also points out that although the Confederate constitution forbade foreign slave trade, international slave trade still existed within the Americas and was no doubt still profitable to some American traders.

Suggestions for Reports or Activities

1. Read about the *Alabama* claims in an encyclopedia or other source. What effect did they have on Anglo-American relations?

2. Read about the slave trade in the Americas. What is Jim Lynn's attitude toward slavery? Why do you suppose he feels as he does?

3. Imagine that you are a sailor on a warship during the Civil War. What might your day-to-day existence be like?

4. What was the British attitude toward the American Civil War? Try researching the *Times* of London for editorial opinion.

Unto This Hour, by Tom Wicker.
New York: Viking, 1984. 642p. (1, 2)

The background of this lengthy novel is the battle of August 28-30, 1862, known as Second Manassas or Second Bull Run. Portrayed from the viewpoints of men of both armies, the battle is an exercise in bloody confusion. A counterpoint to the fighting is provided by brief glimpses of life on a rich plantation in South Carolina and the fortunes of a poor white family in northern Virginia close to the battle site. Occasional impartial observers—a photographer from Atlanta, a British correspondent—strive to record the truth for posterity.

Comment

Interspersed among the fictional characters are the famous Civil War generals: Jackson, Lee, Longstreet, Stuart, McClellan, and Pope. President Lincoln himself makes brief appearances. The main impact of the book, however, is in its depiction of the horrors of hand-to-hand combat and of the unbearably primitive medical practices. There a few adult sexual scenes.

Suggestions for Reports or Activities

1. Check your school or town library for accounts of this battle by Northern and Southern sympathizers (contemporary, if possible). How do they differ? Which appear to you to be more convincing?

2. Imagine the reactions of either Amy Arnall or Missy Brace when she learns of her man's death. How would each of them cope?

3. Contrast the rationale of the men of the North—fighting to prevent the South from seceding—with that of the men of the South—fighting to repel

an invader and preserve their life-style. Given the greater emotional power of the latter, why was the South unable to win in the end?

Which Way Freedom? by Joyce Hansen.
New York: Walker, 1986. 120p. (3)
     It is April, 1864, and Obi, a former slave, is a private serving in the Union army with the Sixth U.S. Artillery of Colored Troops, Thirteenth Tennessee Battalion. Thinking back to the early days of the war, he reminisces about how he got where he is now. He remembers the time when he was a slave on the Jennings farm, with Easter and little Jason; then he and Easter were sent to the Phillips plantation. He remembers their escape, with Easter dressed like a boy, and Obi carrying the old man, Buka, on his back. Obi hoped to find his mother, Lorena, but this has not been possible. And now, after emancipation, he is a soldier, and earning wages. But is this freedom? After surviving the bloody battle of Fort Pillow, Obi is determined to find Easter and Jason, and perhaps to go North with his new friend, Thomas. Perhaps someday he will know what freedom really means.

Comment
     In reading about the aspirations and adventures of one young slave who finds his way to freedom, there is a good deal of information about life and times during the Civil War. For example, students will learn that some southern farms were small, with very few slaves (there were only three on the Jennings farm, in contrast to the large Phillips plantation). The Confederate soldiers at times forced owners to send their slaves to work for the army; other slaves saw action when they had to accompany their soldier masters. Like Obi, there were many black soldiers who fought in the Civil War (over 200,000, according to an author's note).

Suggestions for Reports or Activities
     1. Find information about blacks in the Civil War. Where did they serve? Were there blacks with the Confederate forces as well as in the Union army? In the story, Daniel is asked to spy for the Union. Can you find any information about blacks as spies?
     2. What did Buka mean when he told Obi that freedom was "in your own mind"?
     3. What do you suppose happened to Obi after the end of the story? Create an additional last chapter. Did he find Easter and Jason? Did he ever find Lorena? Did he go North or stay in the South? What possibilities for work did he have?

A Woman Called Moses, by Marcy Heidish.
Boston: Houghton Mifflin, 1976. 306p. (2)

Although this book contains some objectionable language and sugges-
tive scenes, the subject matter—the life of Harriet Tubman—is important and
interesting. Born into slavery, Harriet knew at an early age that she had to
be free. Her many years of hard work as a slave to cruel owners and overseers
included a blow to the head from which she almost died. Harriet finally
escaped from slavery. Soon she began working as a guide on the Underground
Railroad, a secret route followed by slaves running away to the North. Heidish describes several of Harriet's trips, making them a composite of people
and experiences.

Comment

The reader gains from this narrative a genuine sense of the ordeal which
the escaping slaves had to endure. The trips were difficult, food scarce, and
capture always imminent. Historical events such as John Brown's rebellion
and defeat are described with feeling and confusion from Harriet's point of
view. The risks experienced by Quakers and other sympathizers are noted,
along with the death and destruction justified by the promise of freedom.

Suggestions for Reports or Activities

1. Why was Harriet Tubman called "Moses"? What aspects of her life
and work reminded people of the biblical story of Moses?

2. Write a description of a day in the life of a runaway slave. How does
that person feel? What hopes and plans does the person have? What fears does
the person experience?

3. Research Harriet Tubman's life. What details can you add to the story
as presented in this book? What part, for instance, did she play in the Civil
War? What did she have to do before she received a pension. Why?

IV

WESTWARD EXPANSION
AND THE NATIVE
AMERICAN RESPONSE

Arrest Sitting Bull, by Douglas C. Jones.
New York: Scribner, 1977. 249p. (1)

Willa Mae Favory has lived on the frontier all her life. She has always felt at home in the wilderness settlements, even in the farthest outposts, but teaching at the Standing Rock Agency makes her uneasy. Sitting Bull is here, and his role in perpetuating the ghost dance makes him a key figure in a volatile situation. To the Sioux, ghost dancing is the final hope for a return to the life-style of their ancestors. To the white man, it is a dangerous precursor to Indian uprisings. The order to arrest Sitting Bull forces a confrontation of the opposing factions, and Willa Mae finds herself caught up in the struggle of two widely diverse societies.

Comment

Although it is impossible to rewrite history to create a happier ending, this novel reveals the complexity of the situation. The perspectives of the white and the red men are artfully interwoven, and the far-reaching impact of the event of Sitting Bull's arrest is vividly reflected through its effect on the individuals cast in this drama. This fictionalized account is an accurate retelling of fact and a powerful statement about the lives of the people who made up the societies involved.

Suggestions for Reports or Activities

1. Write a letter from Willa Mae Favory to the family she is returning to explaining why she has spent the years working with Indians and why she has suddenly decided to return home.

2. Write a history of the ghost dance. Include the effect that Sitting Bull's death had on it.

3. In an essay, describe the last years of Sitting Bulls's life and the role of his life and death on Indian-white relationships.

Beyond the Divide, by Kathryn Lasky.
New York: Macmillan, 1983. 154p. (1, 2)

When her father decides that he can no longer endure the shunning inflicted on him by the Amish community for a seemingly minor infraction and that he must leave, Meribah goes with him. They join a wagon train heading for California, not looking for gold, says Meribah, but for something else. The cheerful and optimistic beginning of the journey deteriorates as personalities clash, supplies run out, and illness and violence develop. Meribah discovers that life outside the secure Amish bounds is not as free as she had thought. When her fashionable new friend Serena is raped by a ne'er-do-well, Meribah is horrified by community reaction. When she and her father are left behind by the party because of her father's severe illness, Meribah realizes that she must be able to depend on herself not only to survive but also to live.

Comment

In addition to introducing some of the ideals of the Amish, this story affords an experience of the life of people on their way west during the Gold Rush days. Readers will learn of the preparations, the supplies needed, the importance of skills such as wainwrighting, and knowledge of herbal medicine. Good humor and patience ran out, along with other essential supplies, giving way to selfishness and violence. Meribah's determination to find her own life is an example of the fortitude of pioneer women.

Suggestions for Reports or Activities

1. Find out about the Amish in America. Where did the original Amish people come from? Why do they continue to live apart? What values have continued since Meribah's day? What lessons can our larger society learn from the Amish?

2. Read about the Gold Rush. Was it a dream come true or a sad disappointment to most seekers?

3. What chances would Meribah have for finding her way back to the Valley of the Fontenelle? Write a paper describing the hardships she might encounter and how she might deal with them. Why did she choose this place?

The Big Sky, by A. B. Guthrie.
Boston: Houghton Mifflin, 1947. 386p. (2, 3)

Seventeen-year-old Boone Caudill is running from the law and from his father. (Boone has been in a serious fight, and when his dad threatens him with the usual beating, Boone knocks him out.) Taking off toward St. Louis, Boone finds a firm friend in Jim Deakins, a loner who seems to be something of a philosopher. They decide to try the life of mountain men, who travel light, capture or shoot their food, and trap and trade beaver. The book describes their adventures in the wilderness and on the river, many skirmishes with Indians, and Boone's falling in love with Teal Eye, daughter of a Blackfoot chieftain. Can he continue to live as a mountain man?

Comment

The reader becomes immersed in the rough-and-tumble ways of the men who had to find more room, away from cities, building their lives around trapping and trading, making their way among various Indians, managing to survive. Readers will experience the feel of life in the open, the cold and dampness and hunger, scratching for food, sleeping on the ground, being ever-wary of shysters or the danger from Indians. The author also describes the excitement that pioneers and mountain men felt from living in the untapped wilderness.

Suggestions for Reports or Activities

1. Study an historical map showing where different Indian tribes lived during the period of the book. Using an outline map create your own historical map. Include the route of Boone's journey.

2. Can you find information about mountain men? Write a short paper about these adventurous fellows. Do they seem to be the same as the so-called Indian fighters? Could they be similar to cowboys or to the hoboes of a later period?

3. The name of Bridgers is mentioned several times. There was a real mountain man named Jim Bridgers. Can you find any information about him?

Bold Journey: West with Lewis and Clark, by Charles Bohner.
Boston: Houghton Mifflin, 1985. 171p. (2, 3)

Hugh McNeal, bored with his army assignment to Fort Massac on the Ohio River, is delighted to join the Corps of Discovery, under the leadership of Captain Merriwether Lewis and Captain William Clark. Their goal is to discover a northwest passage to the Pacific Ocean. Skilled as a boatbuilder and familiar with the ways of rivers, Hugh is an asset to the team. Contending with the harshness of nature, figuring out ways to deal with Indians, and learning to adjust to the personalities both of the leaders and of the other group members—all of this is part of a great adventure capped by the first sight of the "vast, blue glittering Pacific Ocean spread out before us in the morning sunshine."

Comment

Hugh McNeal was the youngest member of the Lewis and Clark expedition. The author has described what life might have been like for a recruit.

Readers will gain a feeling for the jealousies, petty quarrels, close comrade-ship, and exaltation in times of triumph—all part of life for this small band of unlikely companions, including raw soldiers, French adventurers, and the Shoshone Indian woman, Sacagawea.

Suggestions for Reports or Activities

1. Most accounts of the story of Lewis and Clark assign a larger role to Sacagawea. How does this account vary from what you have read in your text-book or in other sources?

2. Hugh suffered considerable remorse for not taking up for Jack at the time of his court-martial. What other course of action might Hugh have pur-sued? What might the consequences have been?

3. Why was it important to find a northwest passage to the Pacific Ocean? How did the explorations of Lewis and Clark help to influence the course of U.S. history during the first half of the nineteenth century?

Brothers of the Heart: A Story of the Old Northwest 1837-1838, by Joan Blos.
New York: Scribner, 1985. 162p. (2, 3)

This story covers one year, a turning point in the life of Shem, who was born with a lame foot but grew up proud. A brief and unknowing involve-ment in a shady banking deal causes a bitter quarrel with his father. Feeling unable to prove himself worthy, Shem runs away. He finds employment as a clerk in Detroit and then travels north to keep the books for a fur trading company. Left behind at the company's cabin by his three companions, who fear that his crippled foot will impede their need to travel farther for furs, Shem prepares to spend the winter alone in the wilderness. Through the unexpected assistance of Mary Goodhue, an ailing and elderly Ottawa Indian woman, he survives.

Comment

The story presents a picture of hardships and successes of pioneers mak-ing their way west. The essential survival values of courage, honesty, trust, and dependability are shown both in the attitudes and actions of the pioneer families and of the Indian woman who befriends Shem. The book portrays a mutually supportive relationship between a young white man and an Indian woman. Something of the culture of the Ottawa Indians is discussed. The author's use of language based on letters written at the time adds to the authenticity.

Suggestions for Reports or Activities

1. Why were Shem's parents upset about the lot which they had purchased? Can you discover whether this kind of misrepresentation of property was a common occurrence?

2. What can you learn about the traditions or values of the Ottawa Indians from Mary Goodhue? How did her friendship affect Shem's attitudes toward Indians?

3. Can you discover any diaries or letters written by people on their way west? What are the hopes and concerns that these writings reflect?

The Camp Grant Massacre, by Elliott Arnold.
New York: Simon & Schuster, 1976. 447p. (1, 2)
This novel recreates the tragic true story of the massacre of an unarmed Apache tribe in Tucson, Arizona. Weary of fighting and eager to return to its old ways, the tribe surrenders its weapons to the commander of Camp Grant, Lieutenant Whitman, in exchange for peace. However, Whitman is unable to force the vengeful citizens of Tucson to abide by the terms of the truce. Characters who are at once unique individuals and stereotypical representatives of various contemporary attitudes present all sides of the story.

Comment

This book is of special interest to modern students because it exposes a dark blot on American history that has been generally hidden from view. Usually it is the Native American who is portrayed as a ruthless savage; in this case, however, it was the cruelty, betrayal, and hatred of the whites and Mexicans that destroyed the efforts of Whitman and the Apaches to forge a new relationship based on trust and compassion. By allowing the modern reader to relive this episode of American history, this engrossing and powerful novel provides a deeper understanding of the social and political forces of this period.

Suggestions for Reports or Activities

1. Why do both Lieutenant Whitman and Eskiminzin blame themselves for what happened? Was anyone really at fault? If so, who?

2. How is Whitman different from most of the other whites and Mexicans in his approach to the Apaches? How do you account for this difference?

3. Eskiminzin believes that his people must change in order to survive, whereas Little Captain feels it is better to die than to abandon the old ways. Examine a record of U.S. government policy toward Native Americans to see why the Apache was forced to choose between change and annihilation.

Cimarron, by Edna Ferber.
Garden City, N.Y.: Doubleday, 1929. 388p. (1)

Yancey Cravat is an adventurer, a storyteller, newspaper editor, and lawyer; he is a crusader for Indian rights, flamboyant, exuberant, and an altogether unpredictable husband to his genteel wife, Sabra. When Yancey decides to make a new life in the raw town of Osage, out in Indian Territory, Sabra goes with him, reluctantly. Yancey sets up a newspaper; Sabra brings social graces to the town. The discovery of oil creates millionaires among Indians and whites. But Sabra's life has already begun to change during Yancey's disappearances. She becomes a powerful woman in her own right, managing the newspaper, rearing her two children, and setting the style for the community. She is eventually elected to Congress, campaigning for progress, Indian rights, and better living conditions in the oil towns.

Comment

The first Oklahoma "run," when settlers swarmed into the territory, is colorfully (and hilariously) described. The author paints a vivid picture of the growing settlement, of the accommodation of white and Indian population, and of the transforming of eastern or southern city life-styles to suit the ruggedness of the new territory. The impact of the discovery of oil on both the new settlers and the Indians is dramatized. Some of the turbulent history of the politics of the state is briefly mentioned.

Suggestions for Reports or Activities

1. Native Americans in large numbers began moving into Oklahoma in the early nineteenth century. Describe the U.S. government policy which caused this migration. What was the "Trail of Tears"?

2. How were the Indians of Oklahoma involved in the Civil War?

3. The author gives a colorful description of the "run" of 1889. Research the accuracy of this account.

4. Sabra Cravat proved to be a very capable woman, despite her genteel upbringing. In what ways does she demonstrate her ability? Would you give any credit to Yancey for Sabra's development? Explain.

The Court-Martial of George Armstrong Custer,
by Douglas C. Jones.
New York: Scribner, 1976. 291p. (1, 2)

Jones bases this fascinating book on the supposition that Custer might not have died at the battle of the Little Bighorn, that he might have been the sole survivor of the massacre by thousands of Plains Indians. In that case, surely he would have been brought to trial for disobeying the orders of his superior officer and causing the deaths of his entire cavalry regiment. Both prosecution and defense witnesses present their testimony, as the court—along with the reader—tries to reach the right conclusion.

Comment

Was Custer a military genius who had terrible luck? Or was he a glory-seeker with political ambitions? The famous battle comes to life as it is relived in the imaginary courtroom. References to problems of communication between military officers, lack of support in money and material from civilian leaders, and limited training of recruits and horses illustrate the historical context of this incident. Glimpses of life in New York, of intrigue in Washington, and of the mixture of noble and petty impulses in all the characters flesh out the portrayal of an event and a period which to this day retain many unanswered questions.

Suggestions for Reports or Activities

1. Construct in your own words a chronology of the events at the Little Bighorn, based on the accounts in this book. Compare your narrative with an historical report of the battle. Were there any points of difference?

2. Imagine that you were one of the military officers of the court, charged with deciding Custer's guilt or innocence. How would you have voted? Why?

3. Research the lives and careers of the officers named in the story (for example, Pope, Terry, Sherman, Sheridan, Reno, Schofield). Find out what they did before and after 1876 when the battle of the Little Bighorn took place.

Crazy Weather, by Charles McNichols.
New York: Macmillan, 1944. 195p. (1, 2)
South Boy has grown up on his father's ranch, learning the Mojave Indian ways and tolerating his mother's Christian and cultural instruction. This summer his mother is away recuperating from an operation, but South Boy knows that when she returns he will be sent to a boarding school where he will have to be with white people all the time. Then he has a dream—about two hawks. Havek, his Mojave friend, thinks that it may mean something important. It's a time of "crazy weather," a spell of intense heat. Havek and South Boy set off to find the meaning of the dream, to go name traveling. Maybe South Boy will become as one of the Mojaves. But after four days of deep immersion into Mojave life, when the "crazy weather" is over, South Boy realizes he and Havek must separate. South Boy cannot be an Indian, nor can he be what his mother expects. But he is fortunate. There is another choice.

Comment

This story is a tapestry of Mojave legends and practices, rich in Indian lore and also showing rivalries among Indian tribes. South Boy is an example of someone who has come to appreciate another culture, and would like to be part of it, but realizes the pull of his own beginnings.

Suggestions for Reports or Activities

1. What is meant by "name traveling"? What was the importance of finding one's new name?

2. South Boy's hair had grown long. What did the Mojaves mean when they wore their hair "half long"? Why does South Boy decide to cut his hair at the end of the book?

3. If South Boy were going to write a letter to his mother telling her that he would not be going away to school, what could he say to try to convince her to see things his way?

Creek Mary's Blood, by Dee Brown.
New York: Holt, 1980. 401p. (1)

The Indian, known simply as Dane, is half-Creek and half-Cherokee, although he has lived most of his life with the Cheyennes. In his ninety-first year, he tells the story of his family to an interested newspaper reporter. His grandmother, Mary, the Beloved Woman of the Creeks, lived at the time of the American Revolution in what is now Georgia. The story spans 130 years of a struggle to maintain a way of life and to preserve a cultural identity.

Comment

The westward encroachment of European civilization upon the Native American way of life is chronicled through events, such as the forced journey of the Cherokee nation across the Trail of Tears, as well as ordinary events of Indian life. As Dane tells his family's history, he tells the history of his people. This novel presents a powerful and personal tale of the clash between two opposing cultures. It will provide fresh insight into the often overly stereotyped historical accounts.

Suggestions for Reports or Activities

1. Create a dual time line that shows the personal milestones of Creek Mary's family along with the major events of the Creek, Cherokee, and Cheyenne nations.

2. Write an elegy for Dane, grandson to Mary, Beloved Woman of the Creeks.

3. Write a dialogue between Creek Mary and her great-granddaughter, Mary Amayi.

4. Check in a reference source for information on the Cherokee removal. Compare the discussion in the historical source with the presentation in the novel.

Gently Touch the Milkweed, by Lynn Hall.
Chicago: Follett, 1970. 160p. (2, 3)

Janny works hard and without complaint, but she feels taken for granted by her parents. Janny's father and mother run an inn, just where the wagon trains stop for a rest on their way west across Kansas. Her father has named the budding settlement Willard's Ford, for himself; Willard feels confident that there will be a real town there someday. He persuades Mel, who aims to start a newspaper, and Mary Pat, his wife, to put down roots here. Janny is delighted. She likes Mary Pat. But even more she is drawn toward Mel, who seems to recognize that underneath Janny's awkward and stolid appearance there is something special. During that next year Janny sees herself changing, becoming a woman and a thinking person, warmed by what she sees as Mel's interest in her. But when the discovery of gold a few hundred miles to the west casts doubt upon the rosy future of Willard's Ford, and Mel and Mary Pat decide that they must move on, Janny realizes that she has grown up enough to appreciate herself.

Comment

Readers will experience the sense of the expectancy that infused the small settlements as people began to build towns on the prairie. Many people hoped to "get rich quick," as the opportunism of the town planner indicates. The precariousness of these new towns is illustrated by the reaction of townsfolk at the news of a gold strike to the west. The description of Willard's Ford with its new and empty buildings shows the reality of the term "ghost town."

Suggestions for Reports or Activities

1. What are some of the famous ghost towns in the history of the West? Write a paper telling the story of one of these towns.

2. Lupin, the town planner, had a clear idea of what was needed at Willard's Ford. Based on his ideas for Eden City, draw a plan for a prairie town. Why was this location considered ideal? What resources would be essential?

3. What is the meaning of the book's title? How does the title help to explain Janny's feelings about herself?

Giants in the Earth: A Saga of the Prairie, by Ole Rolvaag.
New York: Harper, 1927. 465p. (1, 2)

In this tale of the Norwegian settlement of South Dakota, the author focuses on the experiences of a small group of fishermen-turned-farmers. The first to erect sod houses on their chosen spot of the vast prairie, devoid of trees, birds, and insects, this group of pioneers persists through confrontations with locusts, snowstorms, rival claimants to the same land, and their own bouts of homesickness and doubt. Babies are born, friendships are forged, women go mad from loneliness or grief, and people die before their time—always with the backdrop of a flat land with no place to hide.

Comment

Rolvaag's tale, translated from his native Norwegian, presents a vivid picture of the hardships faced by the settlers. The emphasis is on the psychology of the characters rather than on incidents as such, though there are many of them as well. The various personalities are clearly differentiated. Throughout the narrative, the land itself figures as a demon or troll with whom the settlers must constantly do battle. Some are defeated by the struggle, but some survive to fight again.

Suggestions for Reports or Activities

1. Look up South Dakota in an encyclopedia. How strong has the Norwegian influence been on the development of the state? Give examples.

2. On an outline map of the United States trace the route taken by Per Hansa and his family from the time of their arrival in Canada to their settlement in South Dakota. Note on the map all the landmarks (towns, rivers) mentioned in the story.

3. Several months pass between the last two pages of the book. Write a summary of what happened to the Hansa and Olsa families during that time. How did they manage without their men?

Hannah Herself, by Ruth Franchere.
New York: Crowell, 1964. 176p. (3)

Sixteen-year-old Hannah finds Ellen's and Jonathan's way of life primitive and restrictive. She has traveled from New Haven to visit her sister and her family in a little Illinois prairie village where Jonathan is attempting to run a school for the grown-up sons of homesteaders, young men who have been working on farms, with no chance for education. There are problems with discipline, with too little money, with too much to do, and Jonathan is impatient. Hannah is unhappy and plans to leave as soon as possible. But then Tim Boone and Marcus Drake begin making her life interesting. And there is the mysterious cabin that must be kept secret. Hannah gradually comes to realize that she is not merely Ellen's little sister or Jonathan's responsibility, but that she is Hannah, herself!

Comment

This glimpse of prairie life shows the hardships that determined people faced in accomplishing their goals. The author has had a special interest in the teachers who traveled west to provide education for children on the frontier. The story also describes the Underground Railroad and conflicting views on slavery.

Suggestions for Reports or Activities

1. What were rural schools like in the mid-nineteenth century? How were the teachers prepared? Write a paper about such a school. Can you find any information about schools for older children like the one at Brookville? What about education for girls?

2. At the end of the book Hannah says that she is "herself." What does she mean? What experiences contributed to her coming to this new opinion of herself?

3. Hannah's mother is waiting for a letter that really explains what is going on. Write a letter such as Hannah might write after she decides to stay in Illinois.

4. Start a diary for Hannah.

In the Shadow of the Wind, by Luke Wallin.
Scarsdale, N.Y.: Bradbury, 1984. 203p. (2, 3)

The conflict of cultures and values tore apart the lives of white settlers and Creek Indians living in Alabama in the 1830s. With the Creek traditions already being threatened by white teachings and ways of living, and with the sheer numbers of whites driving away the deer and making Indian livelihood more and more difficult, the Creeks are no longer strong enough to resist. Brown Hawk wishes to accept this and does not want more fighting. Others of his tribe disagree. Caleb McElroy and his grandfather are considered friends by the Creeks. But Caleb is forced to kill Least Coyote who is about to scalp his mother. Yet when Six Deer lies half-frozen and starved in the woods, Caleb rescues him. Caleb finds himself on both sides of the issue and can only resolve it finally by becoming Creek.

Comment

This story probes into the thoughts and motivations of the Creeks as they lost their trust in the promises of the "White Father" in Washington. The author depicts the tensions between settlers and Indians that led to bitter skirmishes and retaliatory strikes, each against the other. The removal of the Creeks to Oklahoma is the story of the fate of many other Indian tribes. Readers will gain more understanding of the Indians caught in the inexorable march of European settlers to the West.

Suggestions for Reports or Activities

1. What did the Creeks lose in their move to Oklahoma? What did they gain? Can you find out any information about the Creeks today?

2. As you read the book did you find that you sided with the whites or with the Indians? Do you think that Caleb and his grandfather were unique in their attitude toward the Indians? Why?

3. How did the "White Father" in Washington justify the removal of the Creeks to Oklahoma?

4. Compare some of the values and traditions of the Creeks as described in the book with those of the settlers. What might settlers (such as the McElroys) have learned from the Indians?

The Keeping-Room, by Betty Levin.
New York: Greenwillow, 1981. 247p. (2, 3)

A social studies project sends Hal into an exploration of the land near his house where a developer is putting up new ones. Interviewing elderly Hattie and her infirm brother Harvey, whose family had settled on the land at the time of the American Revolution, he learns about the Candlewood Curse. Hannah, the great-aunt of Hattie and Harvey, twelve years old at the time, ran away from her job in the Lowell clothing mills and returned home to the farm to protect the family's claim to the land; but she disappeared. Some old magazine stories by Hattie's grandmother provide some clues, and a bulldozer leads to the rest. In counterpoint to this story is the story of Emily, daughter of Hal's social studies teacher, and her possible connection with Hannah.

Comment

British author Jill Paton Walsh commented on the superb sense of history in this novel provided by the interweaving of the stories of Hannah and of Emily. Young readers will derive an awareness of their own connectedness to their family's past, while absorbing specific information about the life of young children in the mills and about survival under primitive conditions.

Suggestions for Reports or Activities

1. Look for information about the clothing mills in New England, and particularly in Lowell, Massachusetts. What can you find out about the plight of young children in the mills? When were child labor laws enacted in the United States? How did these laws affect the lives of children?

2. How was Hannah able to survive without being noticed? What did she have to do to make her "keeping-room" habitable and her daily life possible?

3. Hannah felt that she had to live on the land to keep it from slipping out of her family's hands. Was she correct in this belief? Explain how you arrived at your conclusion.

Killdeer Mountain, by Dee Brown.
New York: Holt, 1983. 279p. (1)

Sam Morrison, reporter for the *Saint Louis Herald*, is in Dakota country looking for stories. He decides to join a group of passengers on a steamboat going up the Missouri River for the dedication of a new fort named in honor of one Charles Rawley. On the way he talks to a number of different people about Rawley, including a mysterious stranger who might even be Rawley himself, though Sam has been given at least two eyewitness accounts of Rawley's death. The stranger, who calls himself Alex Selkirk (the true name of Robinson Crusoe, though this is never mentioned), might, however, be a former Rebel named Drew Hardesty—also reportedly dead. Is Rawley a hero or a fraud? Is he alive or dead? Morrison is determined to find out.

Comment

In this book, the Old West comes to life as many vivid characters tell their own stories: a surgeon and a steamboat captain; Hardesty's beautiful widow, Kathleen; and an Indian girl named Towanjila, or Blue Sky Woman; soldiers and sailors; Indians and settlers; colonels and Canadians. The result is a picture of the West at a time of transition, when relationships shifted and changed, and life from one day to the next was predictably unpredictable.

Suggestions for Reports or Activities

1. Who was Alex Selkirk? Present the evidence from the book to support your conclusion. Explain the evidence to the contrary.

2. The Indian called Spotted Horse complains that the Americans have forced the Sioux into Canada and yet still pursue them there. Is his complaint justified? Check the history of Indian wars along the Canadian frontier.

3. Early in the story Nettie Steever and her husband appear as prospective settlers. What were some of the motives for heading West in that period?

A Lantern in Her Hand, by Bess S. Aldrich.
New York: Grosset & Dunlap, 1928. 307p. (2)

Abbie Mackenzie Deal becomes a pioneer first in Iowa, then as a young wife and mother in Nebraska. Her promising career as a singer is placed last in her priorities, as she experiences life in a sod house on the prairie. She bears and rears her children; lives through drought, hard times, and the plague of grasshoppers; and survives the loss of her idealistic husband. Through it all, she carries the lantern of love for her family and her country. Abbie is a remarkable woman, epitomizing the ideal pioneer strength of spirit. Living to the age of eighty, she sees her dreams fulfilled by her children and grandchildren.

Comment

Realism is the key to this novel. The daily struggles of life in a new land are richly described. Two major wars, the Civil War and World War I, touch Abbie by taking first her betrothed and then her sons away from her. The droughts and plague of grasshoppers that beset the Midwest are reflected in Abbie's struggles to survive and to feed her children. The book in general is a portrait of the strong people who built our country.

Suggestions for Reports or Activities

1. Research the beginnings of the state of Nebraska. What kind of people settled there? From where? What kinds of problems did they encounter?

2. What are sod houses? How and why were they built? Are they any examples left today? If so, where are they located?

3. Although Abbie's granddaughter Katherine does not seem to understand her, she tries to find the missing portrait of their ancestor. Write a letter from Katherine to Abbie telling her why she feels the portrait is important. Then write a letter from Abbie to Katherine explaining why the strand of pearls is also important.

Laughing Boy, by Oliver LaFarge.
Cambridge, Mass.: Houghton Mifflin, 1929. 302p. (1, 2)

Laughing Boy knows that Slim Girl is watching him. She is different, bold; he is entranced. There is some talk about her; Laughing Boy's uncle warns him. Slim Girl has been with the Americans, and some say she is more American than Navaho. Her reputation is not good. But Slim Girl wants to return to the Navahos, to "go back to the blanket." She wants to teach Laughing Boy what she has learned from the Americans, and Laughing Boy will bring her back to the Navaho way. Together they will make a perfect life in the northern desert. Laughing Boy agrees to go with Slim Girl; it's official. Slim Girl wants to settle a score with the Americans, but she cannot explain to Laughing Boy her subtle plan for revenge.

Comment

This book is considered a classic for its sympathetic and informative presentation of Navaho life and attitudes, and for its poetic language. Writing from a Navaho viewpoint, the author describes Slim Girl and Laughing Boy living in a traditional way, pursuing their crafts, silver and weaving. Readers find out about ceremonial dances, the night chant, gambling and games, wedding song, the concept of "hozoji." Gentle fun is made of "Americans," notably in a bargaining scene as an American haggles to buy Laughing Boy's silver belt. Throughout the book the depth of Slim Girl's anti-American sentiment is poignantly expressed. Her unwitting earlier involvement, leading to present tragedy, is a commentary on U.S.-Navaho relationships.

Suggestions for Reports or Activities

1. Why does Slim Girl feel such resentment toward the "Americans"? What does she hope to gain by her relationship with Laughing Boy?

2. How are Laughing Boy and Slim Girl alike? How are they different? How does Slim Girl surprise him? How is he able to explain or excuse her behavior?

3. Several Navaho traditions are described in this book. Check in another source to find more information on one of these Navaho customs. Is the author accurate in his portrayal? What can you add to his description?

4. Read in an encyclopedia or other source about the United States policy toward the Navahos. Write a paper in which you comment on this policy and relate it to sentiments characters in the book reveal regarding Americans.

Little Big Man, by Thomas Berger.
New York: Delacorte, 1964. 440p. (1)

Jack Crabb, supposedly located by the author in a nursing home, tells the story of his early life into a tape recorder. Adopted into a Cheyenne tribe at the age of ten, Jack experiences many adventures during the next twenty-plus years, including frequent moves from the Indian to the white world and back again. He participates in the traditional activities of the western frontier: cheating at poker, learning to shoot, visiting a bordello, fighting both with and against the Indians, hunting buffalo, and so on. Somehow, Jack survives to tell his tale.

Comment

Written in a matter-of-fact style, which does nothing to disguise the outrageousness of the hero's adventures, this novel brings to life a lively and exciting period of American history. It is especially provocative in its contradiction of the accepted version of the battle of the Little Bighorn, where all of the whites reportedly died. It is not necessary to believe Jack's story in detail to enjoy and learn from his "recollections." Particularly valuable are those episodes seen from the point of view of the Indians, often lacking in history texts.

Suggestions for Reports or Activities

1. Find a historical account of the battle of the Little Bighorn. Compare it with the version given by Jack Crabb. How do the two accounts differ?

2. Select any two of Jack's adventures, one which you believe and one which you do not. Explain why you find them plausible or implausible.

3. See what you can find out about the life of Wild Bill Hickok. How much of the account of Hickok that appears in this book is accurate?

3. Jack's story ends when he is 34 years old, but he lives to be 111. Invent at least one more adventure for him during those remaining years.

The Massacre at Fall Creek, by Jessamyn West.
New York: Harcourt, 1975. 314p. (2)

In the year 1824, not far from what is now Indianapolis, Indiana, five white men killed a group of nine innocent, peaceful Indians who were camped nearby. Fall Creek, a settlement about 100 miles northwest of Cincinnati, Ohio, was on the frontier of white civilization. The people who lived there had pushed westward to find their own land, enduring hardships, including Indian raids, before reaching their goal. For many years whites had been killing Indians who were in their way; seldom had they been punished by their communities for their deeds. This time, however, was different.

Comment

Threatened by reprisals from Seneca warriors, the United States government agreed to try the men for murder. If found guilty, they would hang. This book presents a fictionalized account of the crime itself, the trial, and the verdict. The Indians, the settlers, the lawyers for both sides, the accused and their families, all are made vivid and memorable in this moving tale. The lesson regarding what can happen to otherwise moral people who dehumanize those of other cultures or races has its applications today.

Suggestions for Reports or Activities

1. One of the reasons offered for holding the trial was that in the future whites would understand that Indians were not to be killed just because they were "in the way." Was this understanding in fact learned? Why or why not?

2. What happened to the Senecas, the Osage, the Mingos, and the other tribes mentioned as the white settlers moved West? Where are members of these tribes living now? What kind of lives are they leading?

3. Select one of the fictional characters in the story and write another chapter about what happened to him or her. Possibilities are Hannah and Charlie Fort, Johnny Wood, Ben or Caleb Cape, Ora Bemis, or others.

My Antonia, by Willa Cather.
Boston: Houghton Mifflin, 1918. 372p. (1, 2)

The story of Antonia Shimerda, who comes from Bohemia to Nebraska with a family totally unprepared for the demands of frontier life, is told by her admiring neighbor, Jimmy Burden, in an account which covers a period of about thirty years. We see Antonia mourn the passing of her impractical father; learn to do a man's work on the farm at the direction of her elder brother; work in town as a hired girl; fall in love with an Irish railway worker who deserts her; and finally find peace on another farm with a fellow Bohemian and their many children.

Comment

The young reader retains from this novel a lasting sense of the rhythms of life on the prairie at the turn of the century. The compassion of some of the earlier settlers of English and Irish origin for their immigrant neighbors— Czech, Russian, German, Norwegian—is contrasted with the condescension and contempt of others. It is clear, however, that the families of the "hired girls" who send their earnings back to the farm will prosper, while the town youngsters will remain in genteel poverty for at least one more generation.

Suggestions for Reports or Activities

1. Examine the history of Nebraska during the second half of the nineteenth century. What was it that attracted immigrants like the Shimerdas?

2. Lena Lingard, who had a dressmaking business, determined never to marry. Look up the statutes of the period governing the property rights of married women and decide if Lena's decision was indeed in her self-interest.

3. The Cusaks spoke only Bohemian at home, and so the children had to learn English when they went to school. What does current research into bilingualism say about such a practice as opposed to learning English at home?

The No-Return Trail, by Sonia Levitin.
New York: Harcourt, 1978. 154p. (2)

Toward the end of the book, Ben Kelsey reflects, "I reckon I'll remember it for always. And everything we've seen. Even the bad parts, like the stampede and the river crossings and the freezing rain. I'll remember it when I'm old. . . ." For Ben and for Nancy, his wife, the trip by wagon to California along the "no-return trail" is a time of profound growth and a test of their love. This is especially Nancy's story. Seventeen years old, timid, even terrified, dependent, fearful for their baby, aiming only to please Ben, Nancy discovers that she has immense resources as well as physical endurance and plain common sense. In the end it is Nancy who forces the remnant of the group to hold together and makes the joyous conclusion possible.

Comment

This book is based on the true story of the Bidwell-Bartelson expedition in 1841, the first wagon train to make the trip from Missouri to California. After half of the group decided to take the easier trail for Oregon instead, Nancy found herself the only woman in the party. The hardships encountered by pioneers—hunger, cold, heat, Indians, buffalo stampedes, illness, death, personality clashes and disputes—and of the will to persevere to the end provide young readers an inspiring tribute to the indefatigable human spirit.

Suggestions for Reports or Activities

1. This expedition set out for California before the great Gold Rush. They were not in a hurry to get rich. Why did they go? Check in an encyclopedia for information about the earliest settlements in California. Write a short paper on the settling of California.

2. Read about the Gold Rush. Can you find out about some of the fortunate people who actually became rich?

3. One of the reasons for moving West was the lure of new frontiers to cross. What frontiers are there today? Do you feel that it is important for human beings to look for new frontiers? Explain in a short paper.

Only Earth and Sky Last Forever, by Nathaniel Benchley.
New York: Harper, 1972. 189p. (2, 3)

Dark Elk has grown up in a U.S. government Indian agency, away from opportunities to take part in traditional tribal feats of bravery. How will he be able to impress Lashuka's grandmother with his worthiness and win Lashuka's love? In the sacred Black Hills he will ask for a vision. Perhaps if he can capture an eagle. . . .? But soon Dark Elk realizes that the real cause—for himself, for Lashuka, and for all of the Indian people—is the fight against the ever-encroaching whites and their broken promises. The Black Hills were to be forever Indian lands. Now the whites wish to dig there for gold. Dark Elk decides to join Crazy Horse and to "go with the hostiles."

Comment

Written from an Indian point of view, this book describes the frustrations and disappointments of broken treaties and desecration of sacred lands. The book gives insights into the relationships between tribes caught in the turmoil of the white advance. Included are a description of the meetings between Indian leaders and white representatives from Washington shortly before the battle of the Little Bighorn and an account of the battle. Customs and traditions are described, such as the importance for a young man to demonstrate his bravery, the respect accorded older people, counting coup, and dressing for battle.

Suggestions for Reports or Activities

1. This story ends with a description of the battle of the Little Bighorn. Read another account of this battle in your textbook or in an encyclopedia. How do the two accounts differ?

2. Basing your discussion on events described in the story, what was the meaning of the phrase attributed to Crazy Horse, "One does not go to a hilltop for water nor to the white man for truth"?

3. What were the terms of the Treaty of 1868 mentioned on page 18? Chapter 6 gives information on how the U.S. government wanted to change these terms. Discuss.

4. Check in another source (textbook or encyclopedia) for information on Crazy Horse. How does the account in Benchley's book supplement it?

Orphan Train, by James Magnuson and Dorothea G. Petrie.
New York: Dial, 1978. 307p. (1, 2)

Emma Symns has her hands full. When her clergyman uncle falls ill in Albany and has to stay behind, Emma vows to be responsible for completing their mission: to travel by train escorting twenty-seven New York City street children to hoped-for new homes in the Midwest. A minister from Illinois has written that several children from his church died in the winter, and his congregation will welcome new children to replace those lost. Here is truly a motley collection of irrepressible young people who have had to live by their wits, who have learned to be suspicious of adults, but who have been persuaded to join in the adventure in the hope of belonging somewhere. J. P. has been dancing in the streets for coins; Sara has been a prostitute; Bruce and Tom can't resist a chance to fight. Some wonder, "will anyone really pick us?" At their first scheduled stop ten children are selected for homes. But it's a long, long way to Illinois; Emma's worries are far from over.

Comment

This story is drawn from accounts of the Children's Aid Society, which between 1854 and 1904 was responsible for relocating 100,000 homeless children from New York City to farms in the West. The plight of orphaned or abandoned young people who lived an Oliver Twist-type of life is vividly described. Readers will be interested in the depiction of an early train, which by present standards meanders slowly and lacks basic safety measures. The incident involving the fugitive slave shows the conflicting opinions regarding law and justice.

Suggestions for Reports or Activities

1. The development of railroads in the United States is a fascinating study. What can you find out about railroad routes in the 1850s? Note that the children did not board a train until they reached Albany. Ideas of safety were quite different. Research the progress of laws for the safe operation of railroads during the last hundred years.

2. There was some opposition to the Children's Aid Society's method of relocating homeless children. Who was opposed? What reasons lay behind this thinking? Would such a plan be feasible today?

3. There was a fugitive slave hidden in the baggage car. What was the law regarding fugitive slaves? Check in your textbook and in reference sources. Do you feel that the engineer acted correctly?

The Ox-Bow Incident, by Walter van Tilburg Clark.
London: Gollancz, 1940. 238p. (1)

Cattle rustling and murder—these two crimes are sure to arouse passions in Nevada frontier society. Cattle are missing, and Kinkaid is reported shot. The only answer is to raise a posse, find the criminals, and avenge Kinkaid's death. Everyone doesn't agree: Oxford tries to argue, Davies ardently pleads for patience. The Judge warns, "no lynching!" Nonetheless, led by the determined Major Tetley, the twenty-eight men set out on their quest. They find three men asleep in the Ox-Bow Valley and force them to an impromptu trial, with disastrous consequences. Too late they find out the truth.

Comment

This gripping story of frontier justice explores concepts of good and evil. It depicts the simple system of order that existed in the West toward the end of the last century. The book describes the rough life of men isolated from family, lonely for women, amusing themselves through drink or gambling, and quick to band together in a matter that concerns them. Questions raised about guilt and responsibility and the effects of mob hysteria are applicable to issues today.

Suggestions for Reports or Activities

1. What can you find out about Nevada in the 1880s? How important was cattle raising? What cities had been established?

2. The movies often depict the Old West as a society where men took the law into their own hands. *The Ox-Bow Incident,* a highly rated film, certainly gives this impression. How accurate is the picture of frontier justice?

3. Do you think that Davies was too hard on himself in feeling guilt for what happened? Explain his reasoning.

4. Construct a letter Martin might have written to his wife.

Prairie Songs, by Pam Conrad.
New York: Harper & Row, 1985. 167p. (2, 3)

Louisa is a child of the Nebraska prairie, loves its vast lonely beauty, and is eager to welcome the new doctor and his wife who are coming from New York City to settle nearby. And Emmeline is beautiful, though fragile as a flower. Best of all she has brought a trunk full of books, and Louisa is ecstatic. At first it seems that everything will work out, especially when Emmeline agrees to have a school in her sod house for Louisa and her shy brother Lester. And even though she is apprehensive in her unpreparedness for prairie life, and fearful of possible dangers—Indians, snakes, who knows?—Emmeline does look forward to her baby. But the prairie that Louisa loves proves too much for Emmeline.

Comment

The lonely life of settlers in the vast expanses of the West could not be foreseen by all who came there from populated civilization in eastern cities. This book describes facets of daily life on the prairie, including building houses and making them livable, planting, cooking and heating methods, education of children, scarcity of medical care, need for preparedness. It also depicts the feelings of loneliness and fear that drove some people to escape or to despair.

Suggestions for Reports or Activities

1. Consider the lives of the three families in the book. What qualities seem important for families to endure the life as settlers in Nebraska at the time? Write a short paper explaining your answer and using examples from the text.

2. Basing your reply on what you have read in the book, how might you describe Nebraska? If you were going to write to Emmeline before she arrived, how would you prepare her for life on the prairie?

Season of Yellow Leaf, by Douglas C. Jones.
New York: Holt, 1983. 323p. (1, 2)

Morfydd Annon Parry is only ten years old when Comanches and Kiowas attack the homestead, murder her parents, and kidnap her and her mentally handicapped four-year-old brother. The Kiowas go off in a different direction with him. Morfydd, renamed Chosen, begins the long and complicated task of learning to think of herself as a Comanche maiden and later a squaw. Despite her origins, Chosen is valued as a female who can help repopulate the tribe, whose numbers have decreased alarmingly from exposure to the white man's diseases and firearms.

Comment

Told from the points of view of both the kidnapped white girl and the Comanches with whom she lives and identifies, this story shows how people adapt—or do not adapt—to changes in their environment and circumstances. The author offers insights into the reasons for conflict between the various ethnic groups in Texas at the time. Much of the dissension and mistrust between different Indian tribes is attributed to their enforced proximity as a result of the white men's thrust west.

Suggestions for Reports or Activities

1. Investigate the historical relationships among the Mexicans, the Texans, and the Native Americans. Which group of whites appears to be most responsible for pushing the Indians off their traditional lands? Did the tribes respond differently to the different whites? How? When?

2. Explore the role of the whites who became Indian traders. How were they treated by the Indians? How did their treatment change over time?

3. When Chosen ultimately returns to the whites who had known her as a child, her son goes off with his Indian aunt. What do you think happened to him? Did he ever see his mother again? Write another chapter for the book.

Shane, by Jack Schaefer.
Boston: Houghton Mifflin, 1949. 214p. (2, 3)

A mysterious stranger comes into the lives of homesteading Jim Starrett and his wife and son, affecting them all in different ways and leaving behind a challenge. Young Bob Starrett tells the story of how Shane appears from nowhere, wins his family's confidence, and agrees to move in to help with the work of the farm. Shane finds himself in the center of a bitter dispute between Fletcher, the unscrupulous cattle rancher, and the unprotected farmers. Feltcher has a government contract to supply beef to the Indian agent and is determined to appropriate the homesteaders' land to expand his grazing territory. There are some exciting encounters between the good guys and the bad guys. But who is Shane?

Comment

Some of the quality of yesterday's best western films comes through in this novel. It portrays the struggle to hold on to one's property in a time and place where law and order were in the hands of whoever could make other people do what he wanted. The values of standing up for what you think is right, of acting with courage in the face of danger, and of finishing something you have started are presented in an exciting story. Readers will experience the flavor of the raw days in the West.

Suggestions for Reports or Activities

1. The Starretts were being forced to give up their land. What can you find out about the legal rights of homesteaders? What was guaranteed by the government?

2. Where do you think Shane came from? Write an imaginary autobiography of his life before his time with the Starretts. Where was he going when he arrived at their place? What do you think happened to him after he rode away?

3. When did Wyoming become a state? What towns had been settled by the time of this story? Can you locate settlements on an outline map of Wyoming? Where might the Starrett's homestead have been located?

Sing Down the Moon, by Scott O'Dell.
Boston: Houghton Mifflin, 1970. 137p. (3)

When the Long Knives (U.S. soldiers) begin systematically and ruthlessly to force the Navahos to leave their beloved canyon, the people of Bright Morning's village refuse to obey, even when their homes have been burned to the ground. However, after their crops have been destroyed, they give in and begin the "Long Walk" to Fort Sumner and captivity. It is a time of suffering and sadness. But Bright Morning, determined to return to the canyon, convinces Tall Boy, her husband, that they can live in freedom. Through some risky maneuvers they make their way back despite the tremendous odds against them.

Comment

U.S. government policies toward Native Americans which seemed justified at the time but are difficult to accept today are described, along with the picture of the unquenchable spirit of the Navahos who maintain their traditions and celebrate life despite privation and cruel treatment.

Suggestions for Reports or Activities

1. At the time of the story why did the U.S. government force the Navahos to leave their homes? What effect has this had on the history of the Navahos since that time?

2. From the descriptions in the book what can you learn about the Navaho attitude toward nature and the environment?

3. Bright Morning participated in a "womanhood ceremony." Describe the tasks she had to perform. Why do you think the author included this ceremony in the story?

The Snowbird, by Patricia Calvert.
New York: Scribner, 1980. 146p. (2)

Willie Bannerman admits she's out of step, "marching left when every-one else is marching right." Maybe that's because she has inherited her parents' gift for dreaming and telling. Spunky, high-spirited, and clever with words, she plans to be a writer. Orphaned after the fire destroys their parents' newspaper plant, Willie and her young brother, T.J., are sent by train from Tennessee to the Dakota Territory to live with their father's brother, Uncle Randall, and his flamboyant redheaded wife, Belle. Belle, too, is a dreamer, making the best of her life on the prairie, dreaming of a mansion to replace their sod house. The birth of a silvery foal the night that Willie and T.J. arrive seems to be a good omen. Willie names the foal Snowbird, sensing that there is something different about this foal, just as she knows she is different, too, "caught between being and becoming." The story is her journal.

Comment

Prairie life is portrayed as harsh but manageable and the people as tough, persistent, and full of hope despite disappointments. Readers will experience some facets of everyday existence, such as the sod house, the one-room school, the itinerant preacher, the loss of a newborn baby, and the appreciation of small joys. There is also an awareness of new immigrants arriving, confident in the promise of the new life. Even though the Snowbird vanishes, and Belle also leaves, the reader knows that here in the Dakota Territory things will work out for Willie.

Suggestions for Reports or Activities

1. Imagine that you are Willie, writing a letter about the Dakota Territory, trying to impress your friend Beth Ellen back in Tennessee. What would you include? What would you omit?

2. Check in an encyclopedia or other source for information on the settling of the Dakota Territory. What were its boundaries? When did whites move into the area? Where did they come from?

3. Select one facet of life in the territory, such as the sod house or the school or the farm. Write a short paper.

4. What do you think is the significance of the Snowbird? How is the foal related to Willie? To Belle?

The Sodbuster Venture, by Charlene Joy Talbot.
New York: Atheneum, 1982. 194p. (3)

Glad to be out of her sister's house, thirteen-year-old Maud has been taking care of gravely ill Mr. Nelson. At the point of death Mr. Nelson asks Maud to persuade his fiancée, Belle Warren (at that very moment on her way from the East for their wedding) to stay and to try to make a go of his claim. He wants her to farm the land for one year. Belle arrives just in time for Mr. Nelson's funeral. Bravely she decides that she will try to carry out his wishes, and Maud is happy to stay on and help her. Certain that a woman cannot possibly manage, the Coddington brothers, drunken ne'er-do-wells, plot to claim the land for themselves. Maud helps Belle to get to the land office first and officially register her right to her fiancé's claim. Belle and Maud together endure despite the grasshopper infestation, cattle disease, endless dust, the long winter, and the harassment of the Coddington brothers. And there is some unexpected help as Maud makes a new friend.

Comment

Maud and Belle demonstrate the brave spirit, determination and physical endurance of hardy pioneer women. A good picture of early life in Kansas, this book provides readers a sense of the mushrooming growth of the state as Civil War veterans thronged in to claim their promised 160 acres.

Suggestions for Reports or Activities

1. Check an encyclopedia for information on the early history of Kansas. Where did the settlers come from? What can you find out about the government promise of land? When did Kansas become a state? How many people had to live in an area before it could achieve statehood?

2. Belle Warren came from Maine to live on the prairie. In what ways was her life different from what she had known before?

3. Maud at thirteen had some very adult responsibilities. Compare her life with that of a teenager in the United States today. Some teenagers have more responsibilities than others. Write a short paper on how Maud's life is different from yours.

4. List ten adjectives to describe Maud. Write a character sketch of Maud using these adjectives and pointing out sections of the book which demonstrate these character traits.

Streams to the River, River to the Sea, by Scott O'Dell. Boston: Houghton Mifflin, 1986. 191p. (2)

Sacagawea, the young Indian woman who aided the expedition of Lewis and Clark, tells her story. Kidnapped from her own Shoshone village by neighboring enemy tribesmen and betrothed to the son of their chief, she is given away in a game of chance to become a second wife to Charbonneau, a half-Sioux, half-French trader. The Shoshone thought his friendship was important for the sake of trade. Sacagawea's life changes when Captains Lewis and Clark, leading a U.S. government search for a northwest passage to the Pacific, hire Charbonneau for his knowledge of the rivers and Sacagawea for her familiarity with the ways of Indians whose lands the group must traverse. This story shows the expedition as Sacagawea experiences it, a young wife treated hardly better than a slave, caring for her baby and finding herself falling in love with Captain Clark.

Comment

The author states that he has relied on the journals of Lewis and Clark. He has chosen to emphasize the role of Sacagawea, positing a possible romantic link between Clark and his Indian interpreter. The inclusion of the black member of the group, Ben York (actually Clark's slave), helps to document the generally unknown role blacks played in important historical events. The study of flora and fauna on the route was part of the trip's purpose. The importance of good relations with the Indians in order to accomplish the goals of the young United States is indicated.

Suggestions for Reports or Activities

1. How does this description of Sacagawea's role in the Lewis and Clark expedition correspond with the information in your textbook? What additional information can you discover in an encyclopedia or other source?

2. Why did Captain Lewis want to gather specimens of plant and animal life? What other purposes did the expedition have besides locating a route to the Pacific?

3. Trace on an outline map the route of Lewis and Clark. Include the areas where different Indians mentioned in the book lived.

4. Can you find data to document the role of French fur traders in exploring the west? Write a short paper on your findings.

Wait for Me, Watch for Me, Eula Bee, by Patricia Beatty.
New York: Morrow, 1978. 221p. (2, 3)

Only Lewallen and his four-year-old sister Eula Bee survive the Comanche attack on the Collier family's west Texas farm. Carried off to the Indian camp, Lewallen becomes the property of Many Horses, leader of the war party. Eula Bee is given to another chief and kept separated from her brother. But Lewallen is determined to find a way for both to be freed. When he instinctively saves Many Horses from a buffalo stampede, he is rewarded by being allowed to lead the horses to pasture. Lewallen seizes this chance to escape, but when he returns a year later to rescue Eula Bee he is dismayed by her response.

Comment

The author explains in a note that the Comanches and Kiowas pillaged Texas villages and carried off white captives who were sometimes traded for goods and sometimes bought back by their families. But many remained with their captors, becoming members of the tribe. The book allows readers to see several facets of life in Texas during the Civil War, from different points of view: for example, Confederate and Union soldiers, Indians from two different tribes, Comancheros, and settlers. Some Indian traditions are described, such as the importance of hair to the Kiowa braves. In cutting off Small Wolf's braid, Lewallen destroyed a prized symbol of manhood.

Suggestions for Reports or Activities

1. Explain why Grass Woman remained loyal to Many Horses. Why would it have been easy for Eula Bee to have become part of the tribe? What would be the advantages in being regarded as an Indian?

2. Find information on the relationships between white settlers, Indians, and Mexicans in Texas at the time of the story. What was the reason for the Colliers' feelings against the Cabrals? Who were the Comancheros? How did their activities affect Indian-settler relationships?

3. What customs and traditions of the Comanches are described?

The Way West, by A. B. Guthrie.
New York: Sloan, 1949. 340p. (1)

"Do you want to sit in a chair and let others make history?" Lije Evans answers the challenge, persuading his wife to leave behind their peaceful Missouri farm and join the wagon train heading west. On to Oregon! The venture yokes together an assorted group, with different yearnings and reasons for making the trip; Dick Summers, the mountain man, experienced, solitary; Reverend Weatherby, tolerated by most. The young Fairmans looking for a healthy climate for their sickly son. Mercy McBee, sixteen years old, unwittingly the object of Curt Mack's desire, and loved by seventeen-year-old Brownie Evans who comes to her rescue by marrying her. This Pulitzer Prize-winning novel records the day-to-day tedium and occasional excitement, the dangers lived through, the sorrows endured, and at last, "Hurrah for Oregon!"

Comment

Here is a fine picture of the way a wagon train got started: finding enough of the right people to go; electing a governing council; establishing rules; taxes; punishments; amounts of provisions per person. The description of the journey itself, the boredom and seeming endlessness, the weather and Indians, the fears and concerns of individuals, and the way people had to adjust to each other, and care for each other provides readers with an inside look at how determined people, some leaders, others following along, rolled the United States to its farthest borders.

Suggestions for Reports or Activities

1. Why did the various characters in this book join the wagon train to Oregon?

2. Describe the preparation for a journey west by wagon. Rank the activities according to importance, and give the reasons for your ranking.

3. Plot a map of the route taken, including the stops on the way. What factors had to be considered in planning the route?

4. Dick Summers was a strange person. Explain his role in the expedition.

Young Pioneers, by Rose Wilder Lane.
New York: McGraw-Hill, 1976 (published in 1933 as *Let the Hurricane Roar*). 152p. (3)

Eighteen-year-old Charles and his young bride Caroline set off into the Dakota Territory to seek a homestead. On the lonely prairie they have a dugout to live in, a barn, fifty acres of sod already broken for plowing, and a creek with two wild plum trees. In five years, if they stay and work the land, they will have clear title to their claim. Their baby is born on Caroline's seventeenth birthday, congenial neighbors begin building half a mile away, and Charles' wheat promises a rich harvest—until the grasshoppers. Forced to seek work back in the East, Charles leaves Caroline and baby Charles John. But no one expects that she will have to face the winter alone.

Comment

This book poignantly describes the sturdy determination and hopeful outlook of young pioneers in the face of severe privation and loneliness. Living by their own ingenuity and hard work, they learned to deal with bitter cold and blizzards, heat and fierce winds, wolves, the threat of claim-jumpers taking over their land, and unexpected disasters such as the grasshopper infestation. Caroline's bravery is a testimony to the survival qualities of women who settled the West.

Suggestions for Reports or Activities

1. Caroline wrote a letter to Charles that she could not mail. She might have kept a diary of that lonely time. Create a diary for Caroline.

2. Check into the regulations regarding homesteading during the mid-nineteenth century. Can you find information on the growth of population in the Dakota Territory?

3. The Svensons came from Sweden. From where did other settlers come to the Dakota Territory?

4. Two types of houses are described in the story. Find out about how sod shanties and dugouts were constructed. There are some details given in the book. Look for additional information in another source.

V

IMMIGRATION, INDUSTRIALIZATION, URBANIZATION

After the Dancing Days, by Margaret I. Rostkowski.
New York: Harper & Row, c1986. 217p. (2)

His face is so horribly burned that Annie is repulsed. But gradually she learns to accept Andrew for himself. Despite her mother's firm objections, Annie spends her summer days assisting at the soldiers' hospital where her father, a doctor, is treating wounded World War I veterans. Annie finds in Andrew a true friend; her caring draws him out of his shell and helps him to realize that life is still worthwhile. Andrew helps her find out what really happened to her favorite Uncle Paul, who did not return from the war. Annie matures over the summer. Her experience at the hospital makes her aware of the reality that, for some people, the war will never end.

Comment

This story, set in a small midwestern town, dramatizes the long-term effect of war both on those who had to fight and those who did not. The townspeople's narrowly patriotic feelings are expressed in the war memorial, the parade, and their reactions to the wounded veterans. Annie's mother's attitudes seem to typify those of many people who would rather look the other way than be involved with either painful memories or present suffering. Descriptions of life in the trenches give a poignant picture of the day-to-day existence of foot soldiers during World War I.

Suggestions for Reports or Activities

1. Look up information on the Purple Heart. Write a short paper on its history and how one qualifies to receive it.

2. Andrew mentions fighting at Belleau Wood. Look up this battle in your textbook or other source. Where were the important scenes of fighting in France during World War I? Draw a simple map locating these places.

85

3. What is a hero? Was Annie's uncle less of a hero than Andrew? Explain.

4. What is the significance of the title? How does Andrew show that all is not over "after the dancing days"?

April Harvest, by Lillian Budd.
New York: Duell, 1959. 309p. (1, 2)

Seventeen-year-old Sigrid, daughter of Swedish immigrants, orphaned and alone after the death of her father, is determined to be self-sufficient. Rejecting help from neighbors, she figures out a plan to keep her family's house; establishes contact with her long-lost grandmother in Sweden; rescues her friends' son Michael in the disastrous boating accident that kills his parents; nurses her pastor's wife during her terminal illness; and bravely breaks off plans for what she is sure will be an unsuccessful marriage. In a stroke of good fortune, through winning a writing contest (based on her father's diaries), Sigrid has enough money to visit her Swedish relatives. There she discovers a surprising fact concerning her treasured blue wool shawl and unravels some family history.

Comment

Of most significance is the picture of immigrants becoming part of American society. The prejudice experienced by the Swedish is described in Sigrid's father's journals. Newcomers established close communities where they could give support to each other, as shown in the way that Sigrid's neighbors all rallied around her when her father died. Becoming thoroughly Americanized was important to immigrants; Sigrid had not learned any Swedish and knew little of her heritage, as a result of her parents' desire to become assimilated. In the background of the story are the election of Woodrow Wilson, World War I, and Prohibition, and how these events affected the lives of Sigrid's community.

Suggestions for Reports or Activities

1. Using an encyclopedia, research where people from Sweden settled in the United States. When did the Swedish begin to arrive? What was the impetus to leave Sweden?

2. Sigrid's father's name was changed at Ellis Island. Find out about the procedures that took place at Ellis Island as the immigrants arrived. Why were names changed?

3. How might the story have been different if Sigrid's father's name had not been changed?

Dragonwings, by Laurence Yep.
New York: Harper & Row, 1975. 248p. (2, 3)

Moon Shadow tells his story. When he is eight years old, his father, Windrider, sends for him to come from China to America, the "demon" land, where many Chinese men have gone to work as laborers to save and to send money home. The country of the demons is strange, and the demons do not like the Chinese. But the Chinese stay together in the Tang village and support each other. Windrider, a talented kite maker, is a dreamer. Inspired by news of the Wright brothers' invention, he, too, wants to make a flying machine. Through a lucky chance he gets a job working as a handyman out in the demon community, and he and Moon Shadow move to a former stable owned by Miss Whitlaw, who is different from other demons. A firm friendship is established with Miss Whitlaw and her niece, Robin, that lasts even through the great San Francisco earthquake and fire. And Windrider continues to pursue his dream of flying.

Comment

This story describes how the Chinese came to America and the difficulties they faced in being accepted. Life in the Chinese section of San Francisco was guided by the old principles as passed down through the generations, but it was also necessary to learn to live in the demon country. This story, written from a Chinese point of view, will give readers the chance to appreciate from that perspective the unfriendliness and prejudice with which the immigrants were confronted. The great San Francisco earthquake and fire are touched on.

Suggestions for Reports or Activities

1. Find out about the beginning of the immigration of the Chinese to the United States. Why did they come? Where did they settle? What kinds of jobs were they able to find? Why were the women left behind?

2. The United States established quotas limiting the number of Chinese immigrants. Write a short paper about this policy, explaining it. How has the policy changed through the years?

3. Read about the great San Francisco earthquake. Write a paper including information about its effect on the Chinese community.

4. From information in the book and additional information in an encyclopedia or other source, discuss the meaning of dragons in the old Chinese tradition.

5. Write a letter that Moon Shadow might have sent to his mother describing his life in the land of the demons.

The House of Mirth, by Edith Wharton.
New York: Scribner, 1905. 329p. (1)

This story depicts New York society and its skewed values and false ideals at the turn of the century. Prominent socialite Lily Bart discovers that beauty and intelligence without money cannot ensure position. Gus Trenor, whose wife has befriended Lily, woos her with money under false pretenses; Sim Rosedale, up-and-coming Jewish financier, pursues her, but she rejects his advances until too late; longtime friend Lawrence Selden cannot resolve his feelings towards her; and social butterfly Bertha Dorset, thinking Lily is pursuing her wealthy husband, spreads false stories about her. With her reputation sullied, albeit unjustly, Lily sinks ever lower in the social scale. She resorts to using her knowledge of society to assist a succession of newcomers to gain entry. Ironically, they succeed while Lily's descent continues. Ultimately, she lands employment in a millinery shop, only to realize that her social upbringing has not equipped her for the life of a working woman. Bereft of hope, she takes her life hours before the priggish Selden decides to propose marriage.

Comment

Having grown up in New York society in the Gilded Age, the author writes with an insider's knowledge. That world was clearly held together by money and the social ambitions of wives. Far from being a closed society, it took in the new millionaires, provided they were willing to spend money on the right things and learn the correct manners. Matchless are the descriptions of the homes of the idle rich, their architecture and their interior furnishings, lending credence to characterizations of the period as "the brown decades" and "the gingerbread age."

Suggestions for Reports or Activities

1. The author stands as one of this country's foremost novelists of manners. What significant manners are dealt with in this story? Do they tell us something of importance about the times? Have things changed significantly in the years since?

2. *The House of Mirth* is clearly a "woman's novel." Not only is the leading character female, but also there is no sympathetic male character. Why is there no such character? Are there ways in which the story might be viewed in terms of women's liberation?

3. Does the author's treatment of Rosedale suggest anti-Semitism? Or should that treatment be seen more in terms of social class than of ethnicity? What was the situation facing wealthy Jews in that period?

The Jungle, by Upton Sinclair.
New York: Doubleday, 1906. 413p. (1)

Jurgis Rudkus, a young Lithuanian immigrant, and his large family come to Chicago shortly after 1900 seeking a better life. They find jobs in the stockyards, which belong to the giant Beef Trust. Then begins Jurgis' broader education. After a series of on-the-job accidents, deaths in the family, and loss of his home in Packingtown, he realizes that willingness to work hard is not enough. Following some unsuccessful strikes, Jurgis is convinced that organized labor cannot cope with the power of organized capital. If working people are to be free, he concludes, capitalism must be supplanted by socialism.

Comment

The story focuses on many of the evils that led to reforms in the Progressive era: execrable factory conditions; false advertising; child labor; adulterated food; prostitution; and political corruption. With its graphic depiction of the vile and unsanitary practices in the packing plants, the book created a national and international furor, speeding the passage of legislation tightening food inspection. Description of the packinghouse workers' strike was based on the great strike of 1904 in the Chicago meat industry. Optimism over the future of American socialism at the book's end rested heavily on the party's growing popularity at the polls from 1900 to 1912 under the leadership of Eugene V. Debs.

Suggestions for Reports or Activities

1. To the author's dismay, the public focused more on his discussion of unsanitary conditions in the meat industry than on the plight of the workers or the socialist message. How do you account for this response? Yet the Socialist Party did make what in retrospect would appear to be some substantial gains. How do the events of Jurgis' life explain the growth in party popularity?

2. Though perhaps not principally so, *The Jungle* is a story of city life. The author comments in various places about the saloon as a social institution. Discuss the saloon as an urban institution. What can one learn about Chicago politics by tracing Mike Scully's connections with government, business, and crime?

3. What role do blacks play in the story? Given the author's socialist convictions, does his characterization of blacks seem to be contradictory? Discuss.

The Late George Apley, by John P. Marquand.
Boston: Little, Brown, c1936. 354p. (1)

George Apley, scion of a distinguished upper-class Boston family, has died. At the request of his son, a famous biographer undertakes to put together his voluminous letters, notes, and other papers to tell the truth about George Apley. What emerges is the story of a man who wants to do the right thing and is capable of flashes of openness, but who ultimately is bound by the patterns of the conservative and self-important society into which he was born. Although intellectually George has acknowledged that that society is changing, that Boston is no longer the personal property of the old families, and that even his own life has been choked by the conventions he would preserve, at the end he is blissfully advising his son on how to carry on.

Comment

The author, a product of the society he writes about, depicts one side of Boston. He portrays the attitudes of the upper-class old families who felt, as George Apley did, that family was foremost, that background and tradition were foremost, and that Boston was foremost. This picture was outdated even then, except in the minds of a select few. This book describes the manners and mores of a class and a period. It shows the inevitability of change as other groups, notably the Irish, begin their ascendancy in Boston, and as children of the old families begin to stray.

Suggestions for Reports or Activities

1. Research the demographic history of Boston. Write a paper on the changes in the population in the twentieth century.

2. Boston has been called the "Athens of America." Why?

3. Why did John Apley want his father's story told? Why did he want only fifteen copies printed? Explain whether you feel that he would have been satisfied with the book or dissatisfied. What would George Apley have thought?

4. Near the end of the book (p. 346) George Apley writes, "I have stood for many things which I hope will not vanish from the earth." What does he mean? Write a short paper on Apley's philosophy of life. Do you like Apley? Why or why not?

The Magnificent Ambersons, by Booth Tarkington.
New York: Doubleday, 1918. 516p. (1)

The Ambersons of Midland, Indiana, have been the town's leading family for two generations after the Major "made a fortune" in 1873. But Midland is changing from a pleasant town to a grimy industrial city of factories, immigrants, civic boosters, and suburbs. New wealth emerges in the person of Eugene Morgan, an old Amberson family friend, who, seeing a future in the new "horseless carriage" becomes a rich automobile manufacturer. The Ambersons lose their fortune and with it their influence. George Amberson and Morgan's daughter, Lucy, long mutually attracted, become estranged when her ideal of the businessman clashes with his ideal of the gentleman. Pinched circumstances, however, force George to take a job as a skilled laborer in a chemical factory. After being run over by a Model T, symbol of the new "progress," George is reconciled with the Morgans.

Comment

This novel is a memorable portrait of the rapid social changes wrought by the first great American Industrial Revolution. The Ambersons represent any family of "old wealth" pushed aside by the "new wealth" of industry and finance in the Gilded Age. Midland is any crossroads that evolved into an industrial city in this period. Most graphic is the description of the dynamic growth of the streetcar and automobile suburbs. Eugene Morgan seems to be a thinly disguised Henry Ford.

Suggestions for Reports or Activities

1. Why does George ("old wealth") view Morgan ("new wealth") with so much hostility while he sees little wrong in pursuing Morgan's daughter, Lucy?

2. The horse and the automobile (modes of transportation) are key symbols in the story. Consider their impact on the shifting urban life-styles of the time.

3. Discuss the major differences and similarities between late nineteenth- and late twentieth-century cities.

Main Street, by Sinclair Lewis.
New York: Harcourt, 1920. 451p. (1)

This famous novel of life in Gopher Prairie, Minnesota—intended to symbolize life in any small town in the United States of the early twentieth century—tells the story of Carol Milford Kennicott's vain attempts to bring about change in Gopher Prairie. Married to one of the town's doctors, she is expected to conform to the values of the leading citizens of the town, the main one of which is acceptance and promotion of those very values without question or compromise. In the end, it takes her nearly two years of living and working in Washington, D.C., without her husband, to come to terms with what she and Gopher Prairie have to offer each other.

Comment

Main Street is not only, as it has often been described, a portrayal of small-town pettiness, hypocrisy, and complacency. It is also a clear depiction of how not to try to bring about change; that is, change imposed upon a community by an outsider. While many of the particulars are not relevant to the 1980s, the conflict of values is timeless. So is the lesson: The impulse to change must come from within.

Suggestions for Reports or Activities

1. Do you think that Carol ever had a real impact on Gopher Prairie? Why or why not? Will Hugh Kennicott be much different from Cy Bogart when he grows up?

2. What kind of war work might Carol have been doing in Washington? Find out about the influx of women into the capital during World War I. How many came to work for the government? How many of them stayed on after the war?

3. Compare some of Carol's concerns with those of feminists today. Which are the same? Which are different? To what extent might college-educated women living in small American towns still have similar complaints?

Now Ameriky, by Betty Sue Cummings.
New York: Atheneum, 1979. 179p. (3)

Brigid Ni Cleary sets out on a walk across Ireland, carrying only her grandmother's cooking pot. Like thousands of other poor people whom the potato famine has left desperate and unable to pay their rents, Brigid's family will be evicted from their home. Brigid will make the trip to America, find work, save money, and send for her family and her fiancé to join her. But first she must face injury, insult, starvation, and disease. However, after surviving her barefoot trek and horrendous shipboard conditions, Brigid is dismayed by the Irish ghetto she discovers in the "golden" city of New York. Swallowing her disappointment, she finds employment, endures hard work, low pay, discrimination, and loneliness. Eventually she is able to fulfill her dream of replanting her family on land newly purchased in America.

Comment

This novel offers vivid descriptions of wasteland Ireland as well as ghetto New York. Although physical conditions are gruesome, the human element that preys on the weakened victims is more fearsome. These unsavory elements, however, are contrasted with the tenacious will to survive that the immigrants needed to truly win the freedom offered in America. This story illuminates the era of the potato famine and the plight of the brave people driven to this bold venture.

Suggestions for Reports or Activities

1. How did the potato famine start in Ireland? Could it have been avoided?

2. Write a short paper on the anti-Irish discrimination in a major American city (Boston or New York, for example).

3. Who are some of the important people in America who are of Irish descent? Write a short paper on one of these.

4. If you can, locate someone who came to America as an immigrant from Ireland and find out about his or her experience. Compare this experience with Brigid's.

The Other Shore, by Lucinda Mays.
New York: Atheneum, 1979. 223p. (2, 3)

Gabriella is struggling with her Italian identity and trying to be an American. She recalls the painful, poverty-stricken time in Italy as her mother waited and waited for Pietro, Gabriella's father, to send the money so they could join him. Now, almost grown up, she lives within the traditions of New York's Little Italy, but she wants more from her life. Even a high school diploma for girls is almost unheard of. But Pietro's harrowing experiences as an unwitting strikebreaker sentenced to prison and his association with Carlo, a philosopher-union organizer, have broadened his vision; Gabriella's future will be what she can make it.

Comment

This book poignantly portrays the suffering of the poor in an Italian village, their hopes for a new life in America, and the roadblocks of prejudice and tradition which made becoming American so difficult. Working conditions in New York City's garment district were appalling, as the graphic description of the factory fire indicates. The family succeeds in attaining the goal of most new Americans: a house of their own. There are some sexual references.

Suggestions for Reports or Activities

1. Check in a reference work or other source to find out where Italians settled when they came to America in the early twentieth century. What kinds of jobs did they find? Can you find any information about the prejudice they encountered?

2. Several interesting traditions and proverbs or sayings from Italy are mentioned. Write a short paper and comment on how these traditions and sayings are similar or different from some in your family.

3. Find out about the Triangle Shirtwaist Factory fire. Was this a real event? Write a short paper about factory conditions in the clothing industry.

4. Gabriella's father was forced to become a strikebreaker. Look up the early history of unions in coal mines, railroads, or another industry. Write a short paper on the problems faced by union organizers. How were immigrants involved?

The Pit: A Story of Chicago, by Frank Norris.
Philadelphia: Curtis, 1902. 412p. (1)

Curtis Jadwin, a successful turn-of-the-century dealer in Chicago real estate, overcomes reluctance and begins gambling in wheat futures in the great Chicago grain market called "The Pit," bringing on financial panic across the nation. Jadwin's pursuit of power and excitement through speculation had estranged him from his beautiful wife, Laura, who had found herself losing out to the Pit in competition for his love and attention. But the collapse of his paper empire, in which he loses everything, real property included, reunites them as they look to begin life anew in the West.

Comment

Most arresting are the descriptions of behavior in the Pit at a time when finance capitalism had come to dominate the nation's economy. The story also contains insights into the motives of those who gambled with other people's money and played other people's produce up and down in the stock exchange. The market collapse and subsequent panic depicted here mirror similar financial crises in the Gilded Age and afterwards. There are also informative glimpses of the life-styles of the era's newly rich.

Suggestions for Reports or Activities

1. The author seems to be saying that Jadwin is at the mercy of the laws of supply and demand, forces over which he has no control. At the same time, it is Jadwin, impelled by arrogance and ambition, who brings on the market collapse. Discuss the relation of the individual (Jadwin) to social forces (the Pit and the wheat). How might this book help us better understand the Crash of 1929?

2. The book's subtitle is *A Story of Chicago*. What qualities of urban life are represented by the Pit? What qualities are represented in Jadwin? Laura? Cortness? How did Chicago differ from other cities?

3. This is a story about women as well as men. Are the women here liberated women? What do Laura, Aunt Wess, and Mrs. Cressler tell us about women's roles and attitudes at that time?

Ragtime, by E. L. Doctorow.
New York: Random House, 1974. 270p. (1)

The lives and fortunes of three families from different backgrounds and walks of life intertwine in this funny and impressionistic novel of the early twentieth century. Mostly given generic titles (Father, Mother's Younger Brother, the girl, the boy, the old man, the colored girl, the brown baby), the characters are nevertheless highly individualistic, even peculiar. They interact not only with each other but also with numerous real personages, such as J. Pierpont Morgan, Harry Houdini, Evelyn Nesbit, Emma Goldman, Admiral Peary, and others. The end result is a story sometimes satirical, sometimes outrageous, but always entertaining.

Comment

Numerous historical events, both major and minor, play their part in this narrative as well: the development of motion pictures; Peary's expedition to the North Pole; Freud's first visit to the United States; the invention of ever-more-elaborate fireworks; Morgan's opinion of Henry Ford; Harry Thaw's shooting of Stanford White over Evelyn Nesbit; the textile workers' strike in Lowell, Massachusetts; and other noted events or situations dot the novel's pages. A special puzzle for students should be the sorting out of fact from fiction, as they are cheerfully mingled throughout.

Suggestions for Reports or Activities

1. Explore further the lives of one or more of the historical characters mentioned. Are Doctorow's characterizations plausible or not?

2. What is "ragtime"? How does it differ from jazz or blues music? Why does Doctorow use the word for the title of his book?

3. At the very end, Doctorow mentions a series of films made about a group of children from different ethnic backgrounds. Read a history of film in the United States to find out what he was talking about.

The Rise of David Levinsky, by Abraham Cahan.
New York: Harper, 1917. 529p. (1)

David Levinsky, a young Russian Jewish immigrant, arrives penniless in New York in 1885, at the beginning of the great migration from eastern Europe. Hoping to earn enough to attend the City College, he becomes a pushcart peddler, fails at it and takes to begging. On a dare he learns the cloakmakers' trade and is on his way. Entering the garment industry in its takeoff stage, he learns to balance risk and caution. Repeatedly underselling his competitors, primarily by using nonunion labor, he rises to the top within twenty-five years. He remains lonely, however, for despite his involvement with several women, he never marries and is without a family to share in the fruits of his labor. Would he not have been happier, he ponders, had he gone to the university and become a scholar or a physician?

Comment

Written by a participant in the movement from eastern Europe to America, the story describes in loving detail Jewish life in Czarist Russia, the ghetto of New York's Lower East Side in its heyday, and the garment industry when Russian Jews began to succeed German Jews in this increasingly important industry. The many sides of New York Jewish life—the struggle to survive, the Americanization process, labor management conflict, the rise of

Jewish socialism, religious conventions—provide the story's backdrop, giving to it the indisputable ring of authenticity.

Suggestions for Reports or Activities

1. What does the story tell us about the assimilation process? Describe the process in the case of David Levinsky. What Old World elements does he slough off in America? What does he retain? Why?

2. The Tevkin family exemplifies several facets of the immigration saga. Is Tevkin a social misfit? Why does Anna spurn Levinsky's advances?

3. Compare the development of the garment industry with that of other industries like steel or oil. Can Levinsky be compared with Andrew Carnegie?

4. New York had its effect on Jewish immigrants, but New York's Jews also left their mark on the city. What hints of the Jewish impact on the city does the story provide?

Sister Carrie, by Theodore Dreiser.
New York: Doubleday, 1900. 557p. (1)

Eighteen-year-old Caroline Meeber leaves her small midwestern hometown in 1889 to start life anew in Chicago. The city has already recovered from the fire and is a major industrial center. The near poverty of her sister's family, with whom she goes to live, and her small wages in her job at a shoe factory do not begin to meet her social ambitions. After a series of encounters and relationships, she meets George Hurstwood, an unhappily married man who becomes taken with Carrie. They flee to New York. In her quest for success she becomes a famous actress, only to realize that despite her material acquisitions, true happiness remains illusory.

Comment

The author, a former newspaperman, displays his vast knowledge of city life in his descriptions of Chicago sweatshops, life on Broadway, and the newly rich. He describes a Brooklyn subway strike and the Lower East Side Bowery with minute detail. Vividly portrayed is the position of women in a success-oriented society of strivers and climbers.

Suggestions for Reports or Activities

1. The dream of success is at the core of American culture. How does Carrie embody the dream? In what ways does she illustrate its strengths and its weaknesses? Was she a success or a failure?

2. Sister Carrie is a novel of the city, in fact, of America's two principal cities. In what respects were they similar, and in what respects different? Discuss the saloon as an urban institution.

3. What attitudes toward women are revealed in the book? Why would this story offend middle-class tastes of the time? What are some of the turning points in the changing moral climate toward women from late nineteenth century America to the present?

The Sport of the Gods, by Paul Laurence Dunbar.
New York: Dodd, Mead, 1902. 255p. (1)

A close-knit black family seeking refuge and opportunity, the Hamiltons (mother Fannie, son Joe, and daughter Kitty) move to New York City from the South in the mid-1890s after father, Berry, has been unjustly convicted of a crime and sentenced to prison. Over the next few years, the city exacts its toll on the Hamiltons. Joe falls in with a fast, sporting crowd, becomes an alcoholic, and goes to prison for murder. Against her mother's ardent wishes, Kitty becomes a singer-dancer in an all-black musical comedy. And out of loneliness, Fannie marries a gambler who mistreats her. When Berry's innocence is discovered, he is freed, rescues Fannie, and with her returns to their home in a small southern town where these victims of racial intolerance and the temptations of the city are sustained only by a fatalistic faith in God.

Comment

Before the great northward migration during World War I, there were few black people in cities. The author explores certain facets of urban black culture, spotlighting the social club and the theater, with their particular social and aesthetic values, prefiguring the Harlem Renaissance of the 1920s. Especially interesting is the portrayal of whites who frequented these institutions; fascinating, too, is the discussion of the role of "yellow journalism" in race relations.

Suggestions for Reports or Activities

1. This story occurs only a couple of decades after the abolition of slavery. How does the legacy of slavery manifest itself in the interracial and intraracial relations of the southern town? Why is Mr. Oakley so quick to accuse Berry of stealing the money? Are the black townspeople justified in ostracizing the Hamiltons?

2. How does the story reflect the small-town bias against the city that was common at the time? Is it a well-rounded account of black life in northern cities at the turn of the century? What insights does it provide into urban black culture?

3. In 1895 in his famous Atlanta address, Booker T. Washington counselled black people, "To cast down your bucket where you are" (in the rural

South). Is not the author of this story saying the same thing? Or does the story reflect a different perspective? Explain.

Streets of Gold, by Karen Branson.
New York: Putnam, 1981. 176p. (3)
In this sequel to *The Potato Eaters*, Maureen, her father, and two brothers make the voyage to America hoping to find a livelihood. Arriving in New York, they soon realize that the streets are not paved with gold, that living conditions are not much better than they were in Ireland, and that jobs are hard to find if you're Irish. Hearing that there is work in Pennsylvania, her father leaves Maureen in charge of the two boys. Maureen finds a washerwoman's position. A chance meeting with the sailor who had been kind to her on the ship is propitious.

Comment
Readers will gain some appreciation of how the dream of a new life enabled people coming to America to endure hardships aboard ship (hunger, stench, sickness, death, unfeeling treatment by the crew). But they were illprepared for the prejudice which many encountered once they arrived. Paddy's bitter hatred of the English, and his suspicion of anyone not Irish are understandable, as is the need for the Irish to stick together. The qualities of determination, hard work, and thrift are portrayed as necessary attributes for success in the new land.

Suggestions for Reports or Activities
1. The book describes the voyage to America. Is this an accurate portrayal? What can you find out about conditions aboard an immigrant ship? How long did the voyage take? What happened when the ship docked in New York harbor?
2. Why were the other women who worked in the Cabot house so unfriendly to Maureen?
3. Why was it necessary for Da to flee to Canada?
4. How can some experiences of European immigrants be compared with the experiences of blacks in America? Discuss in a short paper.

The Tempering, by Gloria Skurzynski.
New York: Clarion, 1983. 178p. (2, 3)
This story is about growing up in a small-town neighborhood close to one of the giant steel mills not far from Pittsburgh at the turn of the century. Itching to work in the mill, Karl has pretended to be sixteen. But he loses his job on the first day. His only choice is to return to school and wait for

his birthday. Meanwhile he begins to notice that things are changing, both for himself and around him. His friend Jame Culley next door is secretly courting Karl's sister. But what will happen when his mother, who has borne a long and deep hatred for the Culley family, finds out? At school there is a new teacher, young and pretty Yulyona, who attempts to convince Karl to set his sights higher than the mill. Karl is infatuated with Yulyona and tries hard to impress her. After an incident in which he erroneously believes that he has found Yulyona in a compromising situation, the devastated Karl leaves town, but he returns to decide about his life.

Comment

In portraying the life-style of mill families in the early 1900s, this story describes a neighborhood where several ethnic groups live, bound together by the mill, and, for most, by the Roman Catholic church. Because they could not imagine another life, young men looked forward to leaving school and working in the mill. Readers will learn about the dangerous work, the long hours, the kind of extortion workers might expect (being told whom to vote for, having to pay to cross the bridge to the mill, kowtowing to the mayor or other politicians). There is also a look at the way people lived in their homes, how they saved their money, how they spent their free time, the closeness and loyalty to family, the ways young people rebelled. The story touches on the rising movement toward unionization.

Suggestions for Reports or Activities

1. Karl's family and their neighbors came from several different countries in Europe to settle in the area around Pittsburgh. Select one of the countries and find out why people left to come to America and in what parts of the United States they settled. Why did many people come to Pittsburgh?

2. Pittsburgh is noted for its multiethnic population. The same can be said for many of the large cities in the United States. From what countries did the new residents come (around 1900) to Pittsburgh, the locale of the story? (You may choose another city.)

3. Andy decides to go to Gary, Indiana, to work to organize a steelworkers union. What can you find out about the beginning of the steel industry union?

4. Who was Andrew Carnegie? Write a paper on his life as industrialist and philanthropist.

Voyage, by Adele Geras.
New York: Atheneum, 1983. 193p. (2, 3)

Crowded in the steerage section aboard the S.S. *Danzig* the diverse community of chiefly Jewish immigrants finds much to bind them together as they share their hopes for a new life in America. Chapters are written from the varied viewpoints of the passengers of several ages and backgrounds. Eighteen-year-old Rachel finds the attentions of Yasha pleasing; can she forget the sadness of her fiancé's death? Now her father realizes that the marriage he is planning for her in America may not take place. Mr. Kaminsky wonders if he should be making the voyage at all; at his age, will he not be a burden on his nephews? Golda will join her husband whom she scarcely knows, but she worries that their baby will not live through the voyage. Mina is concerned about her little brother Eli who seems backward; she fears he may not pass the inspection when they reach land. The trip is trying, personalities clash, there is sickness and death, but there is also joy, and the travelers care for one another.

Comment

The author provides a kaleidoscopic look into the lives of several people in a time between two lifetimes, on the voyage to the promised land of America. Brave thoughts for the future are mixed with poignant remembrances of the past. Preserving the old ways, time-worn traditions, is important to the older passengers; but everyone realizes that life in America will be different. Commentary on the passage to America from several viewpoints affords readers some understanding of the wrenching and worry that so many of our ancestors underwent in seeking a better way of life.

Suggestions for Reports or Activities

1. Different characters in the story had different ideas about what would happen when they reached America. What were some of these visions of a new life?

2. Mina is concerned that Eli might not be admitted to the United States. Could there have been any justification for her fears? What regulations existed at the checkpoint at Ellis Island?

3. Interview one or more older relatives or friends who emigrated to America. What were their hopes and concerns? Ask them to describe the journey. How does a real story compare with the accounts in the book?

VI
THE JAZZ AGE
AND THE DEPRESSION

All the King's Men, by Robert Penn Warren.
New York: Harcourt, 1946. 464p. (1, 2)

The fortunes of Jack Burden, narrator of this story, are tied to those of Governor Willie Stark, a powerful and ruthless politician in an unnamed Southern state. Through Jack's eyes, the reader comes to know Willie's strengths and weaknesses, the attributes which make him great in the minds of his followers, and those which ultimately lead to his downfall. Willie's assistants and family members figure prominently in the story, as do some of Jack's. Believing that the end justifies the means, Willie hurts many people on his way to the top.

Comment

A classic study of the corrupting effects of power, *All the King's Men* offers vivid characterizations of political figures typical of the era. The impossibility of gaining office untouched by "deals" or governing honestly without compromising one's principles is presented as a painful but unavoidable fact. The complexities of living by one's values are illustrated by the life of Judge Irwin, a man who, in Jack's words, had not *been* good but had nonetheless *done* good. The reader should come away from this book with a greater understanding of the choices people in power may have to make.

Suggestions for Reports or Activities

1. Warren implies that major construction projects may be awarded for political reasons. Check the files of your local newspaper for the past year to see whether any such incidents have been revealed in your town.

2. What is your opinion of Adam Stanton's behavior? How else might he have reacted upon receiving the phone call telling about his sister and Stark?

3. Consider the Starks' son. In what ways was Willie responsible for Tom's actions and attitudes? When did Willie realize what he had done, and what did he plan to do to make up for it?

Appointment in Samarra, by John O'Hara.
New York: Duell, 1934. 301p. (2)

Although the book begins and ends with Lute Fliegler, it is really the story of Julian English and the year his life suddenly falls apart. Son of a prominent local physician, head of a General Motors dealership, husband of bright and beautiful Caroline, member of the Lantenengo Country Club, Julian seems to be at the top of his small-town world. When he gives in to an impulse to throw a drink in the face of a fellow club member, however, he sets in motion a chain of events and inferences that leads to his undoing.

Comment

Readers interested in the effects of the Depression and Prohibition on the upper-middle class will find some insights in this novel. The complicated relationships of otherwise law-abiding citizens with the hoodlums who have access to illegal liquor form one thread of the narrative. The entanglements resulting from the need of some of the characters to borrow money from one of their peers form another. A general tone of sexual amorality suffuses the story, despite ardent lip-service to convention.

Suggestions for Reports or Activities

1. What does the title of the book mean? How does it relate to the story?

2. O'Hara details the pairing-off customs of the young people in the country club set. How are these similar to or different from the customs of high school- and college-age people today?

3. Julian English tries to talk to Harry Reilly in his office, but Harry has to leave at once to catch a train. Suppose he had had time to talk. What would Julian have said to him? What would Harry have replied? Write a dialogue for the two men in a style as much like O'Hara's as you can. Then speculate as to how this conversation might or might not have changed the outcome of the story.

Circle of Fire, by William H. Hooks.
New York: Atheneum, 1982. 147p. (3)

In rural North Carolina during Depression times, blacks and whites share much of their everyday life. Harrison Hawkins, a white boy, and his two black friends, Kitty Fisher and his sister Scrap, swim, gather walnuts, but try to avoid meeting up with their cantankerous and prejudiced neighbor, Mr. Bud Highsmith. The children make a new friend who is part of a band of gypsies, Irish tinkers who have camped in the woods. Shortly afterwards, Harrison overhears Mr. Highsmith and a stranger boasting about the Ku Klux Klan and plotting to "clean out a nest of thieving Catholic gypsies" to give a warning to "uppity" blacks. Harrison knows he must act quickly.

Comment

For younger readers this book provides a glimpse of life in a corner of America during the 1930s. According to a note, the author has tried to use the speech patterns of the time, the grammar and the terms of address. (Some perjorative terms are used but in appropriate context.) Readers will gain an awareness of activities of the Klan and of the climate of fear that engulfed innocent people, black and white.

Suggestions for Reports or Activities

1. Find out about the Ku Klux Klan. Why was it started? Why does it still exist? Why is it permitted to exist?

2. What is meant by the term "gypsy"? Are gypsies make-believe people found in books? Are they real? Who are the gypsies? What does the word mean? Where are gypsies to be found today?

3. This book describes several interesting beliefs, superstitions, and customs of people from the tidewater country of North Carolina where the story takes place. Drinking St. John's tea for a cold is one of these customs. List as many of these practices as you can (at least six) and write a short paper telling about one or two of these customs. Then briefly describe any interesting traditions or customs of your own family or community.

The Dark Didn't Catch Me, by Crystal Thrasher.
New York: Atheneum, 1975. 182p. (2, 3)

A sudden change—Seely's family is moving to a house her Dad has bought down in the Indiana hills. Jase Perry says there's a chance to get work there. It's the Depression, and even though Mom doesn't want to move, they have to. And it's tough—not even indoor plumbing and a one-room school. But Seely begins to feel at home, and even begins to like the hills. She makes friends. Even though Seely doesn't feel poor, she's aware of the Depression's effect on those around her. Dad has to go out of town to work and comes home short-tempered and surly. He and Mom argue. There's sadness but there's joy, and Seely does a lot of growing up. When they move on, she leaves some of herself there in the hollows.

Comment

Families coped with the Depression by tightening their belts and doing their best. Seely's family moved to where there was a promise of work. But some people couldn't cope: Jase Perry commits suicide and his wife is sent to an institution. President Roosevelt's program to provide work for young men, the CCC (Civilian Conservation Corps), is described. Seely's family seems strong at the end, despite their personal tragedy.

Suggestions for Reports or Activities

1. Read in your textbook and in an encyclopedia about the Depression. What were some of the programs devised to help people who were out of work? Write a short paper on these programs.

2. What is the meaning of the title, *The Dark Didn't Catch Me?*

3. What do you think happened to Seely after she left Greene County? Write another chapter to conclude the story.

A Girl Named Sooner, by Suzanne Clauser.
Garden City, N.Y.: Doubleday, 1972. 277p. (2)

Sooner, a sensitive little southern girl from the backwoods, is being raised by the Bible-quoting Old Mam, who mistreats her. Dr. McHenry (called Mac) a veterinarian, discovers her and takes her to live with him and his wife, Elizabeth. However, Elizabeth resents Sooner; children at school are cruel; and adjustment to town life is not easy. A sad incident with Sooner's pet bird causes Sooner to return to her former life, thereby bringing Elizabeth to the realization of her love for the child.

Comment

The Depression is an integral part of the book, as the programs initiated by President Franklin Roosevelt serve as a catalyst to Old Mam's actions. She loses Sooner, for example, by demanding money from the Works Progress Administration and the county. The presence of the Civilian Conservation Corps makes her greedier still, and so she chances selling her bootleg whiskey when the "revenuers" are watching her. The hard times and deprivations are presented with sympathy and realism.

Suggestions for Reports or Activities

1. Research the Works Progress Administration and the Civilian Conservation Corps. Find out what they were, who benefited from them, and how long they existed.

2. Interview several people who lived during the Depression. What was different about their lives then as compared to now? How do their recollections of the Depression affect their lives today?

3. Sooner, Mac, and Elizabeth all react differently to the death of the girl's pet bird. Make three columns on a sheet of paper: in the first column list words that describe Sooner's reaction; in the second, Elizabeth's; in the third, Mac's. How do they differ? Why?

The Grapes of Wrath, by John Steinbeck.
New York: Viking, 1939. 619p. (1)

Uprooted from an Oklahoma farm by drought, tractors, and grasping bankers in the Depression of the 1930s, the impoverished Joad family goes west, there to become itinerant farm workers on the large, corporate farms of California. Unwelcome outsiders, wanted only for cheap labor, they are harassed by local law officers and exploited by labor contractors and at company stores. Only the indomitable will of Ma Joad, the help of other poor folk, and the friendly, cooperative federally run Weedpatch camp save the family from complete disintegration. After family friend Jim Casey is martyred leading a strike of farm workers, Tom Joad, the eldest son, grasps the need for group action, vowing to become a labor organizer. With renewed hope, the family faces the future determined to survive.

Comment

This realistic story of the westward-moving "Okies" is an epic of the 1930s, the decade of drought, Depression, and the New Deal. The author, who lived among them, captures the spirit as well as the trials of the thousands of refugee families who went from farm owners to migrant day laborers in a West where there was no more cheap, fertile land. His descriptions of farm labor conditions in large-scale agriculture have been amply documented over the decades. The Weedpatch camp symbolizes the Farm Security Administration's migrant camp program, the federal government's effort to aid seasonal farm workers.

Suggestions for Reports or Activities

1. To what extent did the disappearance of the frontier of free land affect the fortunes of the Joads and thousands like them in the 1930s?

2. What light does the story shed on the farm family? How does Pa Joad deal with the situation of dispossession and migration? Why is Ma Joad the center of the family? Why and how does Tom develop more than any other character in the story?

3. What solutions does the author suggest, implicitly or explicitly, to the problems faced by the Joads? How realistic were they in the context of the time?

The Great Gatsby, by F. Scott Fitzgerald.
New York: Scribner, 1925. 182p. (1)

Jay Gatsby, grown rich through bootlegging and racketeering, pursues his five-year-old dream of winning his old love, Daisy Buchanan. Daisy, married to Tom and the mother of a three-year-old, cannot decide what to do. Their story is told by Daisy's poor cousin Nick Carraway, who rents a house next door to Gatsby's mansion on Long Island. Other characters who have major roles are Daisy's friend Jordan Baker, Tom's mistress Myrtle Wilson, and Myrtle's husband, George. Only Nick is aware of the harm that people like them can and do cause for themselves and others.

Comment

The book paints a vivid picture of the careless, sophisticated, and self-centered life led by the idle rich in the post-World War I era. The modern reader will be struck by the characters' lack of attention to anything beyond their immediate pleasure in the form of games, parties, new clothes, and drunken oblivion. Loyalty, fidelity, true caring, and even honest communication seem out of place and alien in this setting.

Suggestions for Reports or Activities

1. Look through a history of the Jazz Age. Were the characters portrayed in *The Great Gatsby* typical for the time? How did the rest of society regard them?

2. Fitzgerald has been described as both a participant in and an observer of the life-style depicted here. Is this true? Check a biography of Fitzgerald to see what part of his own life may have furnished the material for this story. Were people like Gatsby and the Buchanans among his friends?

3. Fill in some of the gaps in the past of Jay Gatsby, formerly James Gatz. What did he have to do to become Gatsby? Was any of it legal? What motivated him? How did he get away with his illegal activities?

King of the Hill, by A. E. Hotchner.
New York: Harper & Row, 1972. 240p. (3)

The struggle to survive during the Great Depression is seen through the eyes of a twelve-year-old boy growing up in St. Louis. Forced by the national economic situation to live in poverty, Aaron is often unsure about where he will get his next meal or whether his family will be locked out of their apartment for not paying their rent. Despite his resourcefulness in earning money and staying cheerful, Aaron nonetheless experiences genuine hopelessness regarding his future. Many adventures and mishaps accompany Aaron's long wait for his family finally to regain a satisfactory life-style.

Comment

The effects of the Depression on an average American family are vividly portrayed in this book, with special emphasis on the problems it caused for adolescents already grappling with the uncertainties of their own personal stage in life. The story indicates how decision-making can be entirely dictated by economic circumstances regardless of people's intent and desire to consider other factors. Students who have fortunately not known true financial hardship should find intriguing and insightful the thoughts of a twelve-year-old who suffered greatly from economic deprivation.

Suggestions for Reports or Activities

1. According to your textbook, what circumstances brought about the Great Depression? What does the novel tell you about the Depression beyond the information in your textbook?

2. Compare Aaron's life-style with that of a modern twelve-year-old. Look for similarities as well as differences.

3. Aaron feels at one point that everyone around him is dying. What events led him to this impression and how did it affect his outlook on the future?

Let the Circle Be Unbroken, by Mildred D. Taylor.
New York: Dial, 1981. 445p. (2, 3)

A sequel to the Newbery Medal-winner, *Roll of Thunder, Hear My Cry*, this book continues the story of the Logans, a prototype of the strong black family who manages to survive with grace in a troubled time. Through day-to-day experiences in the hostile environment of Depression-burdened rural Mississippi, Cassie and Stacey, Christopher John and Little Man grow to understand that for blacks, life is not fair. Their friend, T.J., accused of a murder he did not commit, undergoes the pretense of a trial by an all-white jury; Miss Lee Annie's attempt to register to vote brings retaliation on her family; the visit of Cousin Bud and his light-skinned, New York-born daughter Suzella evokes a sickening and terrifying reaction from local ne'er-do-wells. The adult Logans are clear in their insistence on how the children are to behave in the situation they live in and the family remains strong, even during the tension of Stacey's disappearance.

Comment

The author has stated that these stories about the Logans are intended to show all young readers the quality of suffering and resistance, of determination despite enormous odds, as lived by black people, particularly in the South, in the years before the Civil Rights movement. Readers both black and white will derive some understanding of the foundation underlying today's freedoms. The book provides a view of the effect of the Depression on the rural poor and of the failure of federal farm programs designed to help them.

Suggestions for Reports or Activities

1. T. J. never had a chance. Why?

2. Why was it necessary for Congress to pass a voting rights act during the 1960s? How many registered voters are there in Mississippi today? How

many blacks are registered? Who are some of the important black elected officials in the South today?

3. Read about President Roosevelt's farm policies during the Depression. Why were farmers encouraged to destroy a portion of their products? What were some of the other federal plans to assist people in need?

Manhattan Transfer, by John Dos Passos.
Boston: Houghton Mifflin, 1925. 404p. (1)

The characters in this impressionistic novel are immigrants and old-line Americans, rich and poor, honest and crooked, lawyers and soldiers, men and women—in short, a kaleidoscope of New York City in the first quarter of this century. Many of them meet and interact, sometimes over many years; others become known through newspaper accounts of their activities. Ellen Thatcher, born on page one, is the thread that holds the story together, even as she changes her name first to Elaine and later to Helena. Her changing relationships with many of the men in the story make it seem that the New York of this period was really a very small place.

Comment

The careful reader of this work comes away with a rich sense of the sounds, sights, and flavors of Manhattan. The plot itself is much less important than the sense of participation in the era. Dos Passos touches upon World War I, immigration from Eastern Europe, Prohibition, unemployment, and speculation in stocks as issues directly affecting the lives of his characters.

Suggestions for Reports or Activities

1. There was significant unemployment following World War I. Find out how much, and what resources were available to people who were out of work. Did the government help at all? Or were the unemployed dependent on charity?

2. Stanwood Emery is one of the numerous characters in this book who drink too much. Write a psychological profile of Stan which explains why he drank. Include a brief account of his life and the manner of his death.

3. George Baldwin decides to run for district attorney on a "reform" ticket, to the consternation of the workers who had intended to support him. What did reform mean, and why were the union people so upset?

Native Son, by Richard Wright.
New York: Harper & Row, 1940. 392p. (1, 2)

It is Chicago in the 1930s. Twenty-year-old Bigger Thomas is ordered by a relief agency to take a job as a chauffeur with a rich white family in another part of the city. He is thrilled to have a room of his own, in contrast to the rat-infested one he had been sharing with three others. but he is bewildered by the kindness shown to him by the family and their Irish housekeeper. Instead of appreciating this kindness, however, he resents it as being directed impersonally towards him as a representative black rather than as the unique individual he really is. It is only hours before tragedy strikes and sets the tone for the rest of the narrative.

Comment

The total isolation—physical, geographical, psychological—of blacks and whites from each other appears to mark this period of history. Some modern readers may be astonished at Wright's depiction of American Communists as the only whites genuinely interested in understanding Bigger, rather than simply patronizing him. The capitalists' hostility to the development of labor unions is also emphasized.

Suggestions for Reports or Activities

1. The only whites in this book who seemed to care about Bigger Thomas were Communists. Research Wright's personal experience with communism, starting with his own words in *The God That Failed*, Harper, 1950.

2. Investigate the relationship of the labor union movement of the 1930s with the American Communist Party. How much influence did the Communists have at that time and why did it not continue at that level?

3. In your opinion, exactly why did Bigger kill Mary?

No Promises in the Wind, by Irene Hunt.
Chicago: Follett, 1970. 249p. (3)

It is 1932. Josh's father has been out of work for eight months. His mother irons in a laundry. There is not enough to eat. Alienated by his father's ill humor and anger, Josh decides that he must strike out on his own. At least that will make one less mouth to feed. His best friend Howie eagerly joins him. Unexpectedly, Josh's little brother wants to come along, and Josh reluctantly agrees. Hoping to support themselves with their amateur musical talent, they hop a freight train heading south. Howie is killed in a tragic accident, but Josh and Joey manage to eke out a bare existence, sometimes begging, sometimes picking from garbage cans. A generous truck driver heading toward New Orleans puts them in touch with a carnival, where for a while they are able to make a small living. But this kind of life does not last. When will Josh forgive his father and return home?

Comment

This graphic picture of how the Depression affected millions of Americans effectively portrays the human suffering. Thousands of jobless men rode the rails, creating the unique way of life of the hobo. People are described as beaten and tired, angry, sometimes compassionate toward the suffering of others, sometimes vengeful toward those with more to eat. Readers will learn of the strain on family relationships and of the desperation of people driven to stand in soup lines, forage in garbage cans, or rob someone of a few potatoes. The author describes the hope evoked by the election of Roosevelt.

Suggestions for Reports or Activities

1. Trace Josh and Joey's journey. What do you think of Josh's decision to run away? Would this be a reasonable option in present-day America?

2. Read President Roosevelt's inaugural address of 1933. What plans did he announce for coping with the Depression?

3. Write a short paper on the meaning of Roosevelt's words, "The only thing we have to fear is fear itself."

4. What were the causes of the Depression? How did the United States find the way back to prosperity?

The Rock and the Willow, by Mildred Lee.
New York: Lothrop, Lee & Shepard, 1963. 223p. (3)

A poor Alabama truck farm during the 1930s is the background with which adolescent Enie Singleton must contend. She aspires to go to college, even though the farm barely meets the family's daily needs. Enie's mother is a soft, understanding woman who works too hard and has too many babies. Her father is hard-working but insensitive to Enie's need for higher education. It is only after her mother dies that life changes for the better for the Singletons. While Enie suffers the sadness of her mother's death, later she is able to begin living her dream of a different sort of life.

Comment

The Depression makes daily survival even harder for the Singleton family. A drought destroys one crop, and food and money are scarce. The family is too proud to accept charity. A drifter (a familiar figure of the time) helps for a while, but he travels on after an involvement with Enie. Through this story, the young reader may come to a fuller understanding of a period in U.S. history still recalled by many who are alive today.

Suggestions for Reports or Activities

1. Enie keeps a journal in which she writes about her feelings, her school, and her surroundings. Write a few pages from the journal that she keeps after she leaves the farm. Include descriptions of her new surroundings, activities, future plans, and so forth.

2. On a piece of paper make two columns. In the first column list all of the reasons why Enie should go away from the farm; in the second column

list her father's reasons why she should not. Which set of reasons makes more sense to you? Why?

3. Research the life of small farmers during the Depression. How accurate is the picture offered by this book?

Roll of Thunder, Hear My Cry, by Mildred D. Taylor.
New York: Dial, 1976. 276p. (2, 3)

Growing up in rural Mississippi during the Depression, Cassie Logan and her brothers Stacey, Christopher John, and Little Man are more fortunate than many folks, black or white, because the Logans own their land. They are a loving, close-knit family, disciplined and highly principled. Mama teaches in the Negro school. There's not enough money from the cotton crop to pay the taxes, and so Papa works on the railroad. They live within the prevailing system of white dominance but resist where possible. For example, Mama organizes a boycott of the Wallaces' store when it is learned that the Wallaces are responsible for setting some black men on fire. But Cassie is beginning to learn that justice for blacks does not exist in this place at this time.

Comment

This story, a Newbery Medal winner, shows that despite the pain suffered each day of their lives in the South during the Depression, black families strove to teach their children dignity. The book points up: the treatment of blacks by poor whites who were also struggling for existence; the faulty criminal justice system; the worn, soiled textbooks given to black schools; the demeaning use of first names for blacks while blacks had to use respectful titles when addressing whites; sly attempts by white landowners to steal land owned by blacks; various methods of making blacks submit to white demands.

Suggestions for Reports or Activities

1. What advantages did the Logans have over T. J. Avery's family? Why did T. J. try to act important? Why did he hang around with Jeremy's brothers?

2. How did the Depression affect the lives of farmers in the South? How did the U.S. government attempt to improve the farmer's lot?

3. The author gives some examples of how blacks tried to resist or to "get back at" some of the treatment they received. Comment on these efforts. Do you think they helped to bring about changes? Explain.

Tracks, by Clayton Bess.
Boston: Houghton Mifflin, 1986. 180p. (2, 3)

It is the middle of the Depression. Eleven-year-old Blue, feeling that he no longer fits in at home, manages to scramble aboard a freight car, following after his big brother, Monroe. Monroe is already experienced in riding the rails to look for work. It's a rough life, Blue finds out. Although they find a friendly welcome among the hoboes, there are also unpleasant characters, like Blade, who is surly and vindictive. Food is scarce, baths are few, and riding the rails is dangerous. Monroe and Blue get work for a while, helping an Italian farm widow whose husband was killed by the Ku Klux Klan as he tried to unionize the sharecroppers. When they chance to witness a group of Klansmen butchering a Mexican youth for courting a white girl, the Klansmen spread the rumor that the boys are the murderers. Monroe is seriously hurt in their escape, but help comes though the brotherhood of the "tracks."

Comment

The adventures of Blue and Monroe evoke the life thousands of desperate men lived during the Depression. The culture of the hoboes is a fascinating part of the American past: the dangers and discomfort of traveling by freight car, the gatherings in "jungles," begging at farmhouses for work or food, friendships made on the road. This book also provides a chilling look at the activities of the Ku Klux Klan, the plight of sharecroppers under federal agricultural policies, and the lives of people in the Dust Bowl. The use of speech patterns and aphorisms of rural Oklahoma adds to the sense of history.

Suggestions for Reports or Activities

1. What was the Dust Bowl? Locate this region on a map. How did the Depression affect the people who lived in the Dust Bowl? Check in a reference source for information on the tree-planting project mentioned in the book.

2. Find out more about the "hoboes." Write a short paper on the lifestyle of the hoboes. Were there any unwritten or informal codes of behavior which hoboes followed?

3. This book includes several terms which belong to the slang of the hoboes. What is a "jungle"? A "bull"? Can you locate any other slang terms of the hoboes?

4. Research the attitudes of the Ku Klux Klan toward unions. Discuss these in a short paper. Does your research correspond to the events in the book?

Walk Gently This Good Earth, by Margaret Craven.
New York: Putnam, 1977. 172p. (1, 2)

The Westcott family is affected by various events in history, starting with the Depression. Close-knit and affectionate, the family weathers all the tragedies and good times that befall them by relying on traditional values. The father, Judge Westcott, is portrayed as a solid and wise anchor who leaves a tremendous gap when he dies. Then World War II separates Cathy from her adopted brother, Angela marries hastily, and Maria becomes a nun. How the family survives as a unit makes for a story of compassion.

Comment

The economic misery of the Depression, the personal and political hardships of World War II, and the social turbulence of the 1960s all take their toll on the family in various ways. At the same time, all are made vivid and meaningful for the modern reader because of their impact on the fictional characters. The Westcotts meet their problems in general with independent yet cooperative spirits.

Suggestions for Reports or Activities

1. Find out what the Spectre of the Brocken is. Write a description of it and of the children's experience with it. How did they feel?

2. Write an article for the People section of the local newspaper about Neal's return from the war.

3. Make a family album by cutting out or drawing pictures to represent family members. Show their development through the years. Write a paragraph about each phase in history to include with the different sections in the album.

VII
AMERICA IN THE
MODERN WORLD

Alan and Naomi, by Myron Levoy.
New York: Harper, 1977. 192p. (3)

Alan grumbles about his parents' request that he spend time with a strange girl, the silent and withdrawn Naomi who with her mother has escaped from war-torn France and moved in with the Liebmans upstairs. Naomi is in shock. She has seen her father killed by the Gestapo. Now she simply sits tearing paper into little pieces. But with Alan's help she begins to respond. She begins going to school with Alan. But her recovery is not so simple. A distressing incident plunges her back into her shell.

Comment

Since America was spared invasion and bombing, World War II was experienced differently here. This book shows one facet of the impact of the war on the United States, the accommodation of refugees from Hitler's Europe into American society. It shows the psychological effects of war experiences on one young person and touches on the damaging consequences of religious prejudice.

Suggestions for Reports or Activities

1. One important anti-Nazi activity during World War II was the operation of the French Underground, which facilitated the escape of Jews hunted by the Gestapo. Read about the underground movement in France. What was the importance of the Paris sewer system?

2. Check some facts on the coming of persecuted Jewish people into the United States during the Second World War. From what countries did they come? Who were some of the people well-known today who came to America as a result of Hitler's purge? Write a short paper telling of the life and contributions of one such person.

3. Would you have preferred another ending to the book? Since this is a story which points to some of the terrible effects of war, is the ending appropriate? Try writing an alternate conclusion.

The Bridges at Toko-ri, by James A. Michener.
New York: Random House, 1953. 147p. (1, 2, 3)

Harry Brubaker, Denver lawyer and reluctant Navy pilot, is part of a naval task force flying jet bombers from an aircraft carrier operating off the Korean shore. Their mission is to destroy the heavily guarded bridges at Toko-ri, thereby preventing essential supplies from moving to the Communists' front lines. The complicated task of landing the planes on the pitching decks of the carriers—which are no longer located where they were when the pilots took off—is portrayed with particular vividness.

Comment

Michener, who wrote this short book while the Korean War was in progress, contrasts the tension and high drama of the war with the apathy and ignorance of the folks back home. At the same time, the war is not in any way glorified: disappointment, despair, and death are daily hallmarks of life in combat. Brubaker, who does not want to be there is portrayed with sympathy, but so are the enthusiastic helicopter pilots, the admiral, and the commander of the air group.

Suggestions for Reports or Activities

1. Brubaker complains that nobody back home cares about the war in Korea. Was this true? If so, why? Check lead articles in national newspapers such as the *New York Times* for supporting evidence.

2. Many American servicemen, like Mike Forney, developed emotional ties with Japanese and other Asian women they met during their rest and recreation stops. Some of them married their sweethearts and brought them home, but others did not. Look into the fate of the Amerasian children whose fathers abandoned them. Who has taken care of them?

3. Write the letter that Admiral Tarrant had to write to Brubaker's family. Then write Nancy Brubaker's reply. Did she understand why Harry died?

Caribou, by Meg Wolitzer.
New York: Greenwillow, 1985. 167p. (3)

Becca's family hovers around the television set as the Vietnam draft lottery begins. The very first date drawn is her brother Stevie's birthday. Stevie is devastated. He does not report for his physical as scheduled; he has decided to go to Canada. Father is angry, Mother is upset, and Becca knows only that she is going to miss Stevie very much. But she is busy with her best friend Kate, and with school, and especially with the My Country 'Tis of Thee art contest for a school mural. If she is the one chosen to paint the school mural, she will win the $100 prize. Becca is determined to go to Canada to visit Stevie, but her father is violently opposed. Becca is the winner, for her proposal to paint a parade with American flags. But while she is painting and thinking about Stevie and Vietnam and her father, she has another idea.

Comment

Conflicting views of the Vietnam War are depicted: Becca's father's conviction that one's first duty is to one's country; her mother's indecisiveness; and Stevie's determination to make his own decisions about his life. Becca is shown maturing, also affected by the war. The book captures the ambience of the early 1970s, with references to Beatles music, smoking pot, and communal living. For young readers *Caribou* is an informative and thoughtful picture of a tense time.

Suggestions for Reports or Activities

1. What was the date of the Vietnam draft lottery on television? What were some of the reactions of people to this event? Read editorials and letters to the editor in your local newspaper. Check also the *New York Times* or another national paper. Write a brief paper on your findings.

2. Find out about the young men who emigrated to Canada to avoid serving in Vietnam. How many went? Where did they go? What did they do? What has happened to them?

3. What do you think about Stevie's decision? Why? Discuss in a short paper.

The Dollmaker, by Harriette Arnow.
New York: Macmillan, 1954. 549p. (1)

Gertie Nevels has finally saved enough money to buy her own piece of land when her husband Clovis goes off to Detroit to work in a factory producing goods for the war effort. Soon he calls for Gertie and the children to leave Kentucky and join him. In the housing project near the plant, this once competent and self-assured woman finds herself overwhelmed by the alien demands of city life. Some members of the family eventually adjust; some do not. Gertie herself sorrowfully gives up the whittling that she used to do for her own satisfaction to make cheap dolls and other objects to sell for extra cash.

Comment

The production requirements of the Second World War lured many country people from the South to the big cities of the North. Most of them never went back. This long and poignant narrative is written with sympathy for the "hillbillies" and their problems. The sudden juxtaposition of individuals from many ethnic and religious backgrounds highlights their differences but also their common humanity. Unions and strikes, fear of "Communists," hostility toward new immigrants, and other issues enter also into the story.

Suggestions for Reports or Activities

1. Check reference works in the library for information on "Old Man Flint." Is there another view of his character besides that presented in this book? Compare what you find out with what is known about Henry Ford.

2. What happened after this story ended? That is, how long were Detroit workers out on strike? How many eventually went back to work? Can you find out what percentage of southerners went back to the South after the war?

3. Write a letter that one of the older children (Reuben, Clytie, Cassie) might have written to their grandmother after the first year in Detroit.

Fallen Angels, by Walter Dean Myers.
New York: Scholastic, 1988. 286p. (2, 3)

Richie Perry, seventeen, is out of high school and in the war. He might have gone on to City College—but money has always been scarce, and now he can send some home to his mom and little brother in Harlem. Richie tells his story, of the camaraderie that develops among the men during the "hours of boredom and seconds of terror," and of the fighting, the narrow escapes, being wounded, and surviving. At first, the war seems something far away, and then guys he knows are killed, even Lieutenant Carroll. To save his own life, Richie guns down a young Vietcong soldier, but getting accustomed to this role is difficult. There are jokes, there is fear, and then there is guilt when someone else is not going to get to go home. Richie and his good friend Pee Wee are lucky.

Comment

This grippingly realistic account shows the day-to-day lives of young soldiers in Vietnam. The events at home—the demonstrations and draft card burnings—and the attempts to make peace are mentioned, but they seem unreal to the teenage soldiers as they struggle to make sense of their being in Nam. The bantering and fooling around, which make daily life tolerable, are in contrast to the fear, the pain, the confusion, the carnage (accidental or purposeful), the courage, and the attempt to understand, which the author describes in the vivid language of young soldiers. This graphic account of life "in the trenches" of Vietnam will contribute to young readers' understanding of the general feeling of ambiguity regarding the Vietnamese conflict.

Suggestions for Reports or Activities

1. What lay behind the United States' involvement in the Vietnamese conflict? Based on what you have read in the novel, your text, and other sources, discuss the official U.S. government position.

2. From what you have found out in the book, who served in Vietnam? That is, whose war was it?

3. Can you notice any changes in Richie as a result of his experiences? Discuss.

4. What do you suppose happened to Richie and Pee Wee after they came home? Write what you think in a short epilogue to the story.

Fragments, by Jack Fuller.
New York: Morrow, 1984. 210p. (1, 2)

During the peak of the war in Vietnam, two young men join the United States military. One enlists by choice; the other is drafted out of college. Neumann, the charismatic leader and natural fighter, and Morgan, the pensive pessimist, bond together in the struggle for survival during their year of combat. As they become more involved in the horrors of Vietnam, however, a shocking turn of events threatens their friendship as well as their lives.

Comment

Told from the point of view of Morgan, this novel makes vivid his participation in a war that he does not understand and cannot justify. The book thus provides a glimpse of what it is like for an eighteen-year-old to leave college, enter the army, and be forced to grow up immediately. Neumann exhibits another side of American youth, that of a volunteer who dedicates himself to his own success and that of his companions in a totally new and alien environment. The complex friendship that develops contrasts the personalities of the two young men and sets the scene for an enlightening look at the Vietnam War.

Suggestions for Reports or Activities

1. Locate a Vietnam veteran in your community: a neighbor, family member, teacher, or person referred to you by your local veterans' organization. Ask him or her to tell you some stories about serving in Vietnam. Compare these to the tales included in this book.

2. Analyze the reasons for the reactions of Neumann and Morgan to the task of readjusting to the "world." Which of them had the easier time? why?

3. Speculate about why Neumann and Morgan became such close friends despite their many and obvious differences. What needs did each have that the other was able to fill?

Freedom's Blood, by James D. Foreman.
New York: Franklin Watts, 1979. 114p. (2, 3)

By the summer of 1964, Michael Schwerner has been working in Meridian, Mississippi, for nearly six months, encouraging local blacks to register and vote. In the company of a new college student recruit, Andrew Goodman, and a native black Mississippian, James Chaney, Mickey drives to the rural town of Longdale where he plans to locate a freedom school in a church. The church has recently been burned to the ground and its members beaten. The three young men decide to hold the school on benches amid the ashes. Then they head back for Meridian. They never make it.

Comment

Freedom's Blood is a fictionalized account of three civil rights workers who were murdered at the very beginning of "Freedom Summer," which brought 600 northerners to the South. A vivid reconstruction of their motivations, their fears, their hopes, and their faith in law and basic human goodness makes their short lives transcend their brutal deaths. Knowing how the story ends does not diminish the suspense of the fateful drive.

Suggestions for Reports or Activities

1. Read a contemporary newspaper account of the debates in Congress related to the Civil Rights Acts of 1964 and 1968 or the Voting Rights Act of 1965. Were there any references, either positive or negative, to the activities of northern civil rights workers in the South? Discuss.

2. What did your nearest large-city newspaper have to say when the deaths of Schwerner, Goodman, and Chaney were discovered? Who was to blame?

3. Write the letter of farewell to his wife, Rita, that Mickey Schwerner might have written if he had had time. What feelings (besides his love for her) might he have expressed, knowing that he was about to die?

Going after Cacciato, by Tim O'Brien.
New York: Delacorte, 1978. 338p. (1, 2)

During the Vietnam War, a soldier named Cacciato walks away from combat to "go to Paris." His comrades set off to find him amidst the jungles and mountains of Vietnam, but Cacciato is elusive. Told from the point of view of Private Paul Berlin, this story focuses on the close relationship between the group's actual wartime adventures and Paul's fantasies about following Cacciato across 8,600 miles to the peace and security of Paris. Confined to an observation tower, Paul remembers the ways his friends have died, one by one, as he envisions how Cacciato might actually make it to Paris after all.

Comment

By juxtaposing the two types of experiences, real and imagined, the author manages to make both of them vivid and convincing. Both illuminate the relationships among the men and between them and their officers, their encounters with the Vietnamese, and their constant inner conflicts as a result of their only fragmentary understanding of their purpose in being in Vietnam at all.

Suggestions for Reports or Activities

1. At what point in the story did you realize that the men were not truly on the road to Paris? List some of the clues provided by the author that indicate the imaginary nature of the trip.

2. One of the incidents recounted by Paul has to do with the men's blowing up a tunnel that their lieutenant is exploring. Do some research in your local newspaper files for the late 1960s or early 1970s (or check the microfilms of the *New York Times*) for news of similar true incidents.

3. On a map of Europe and Asia trace the route followed by the men in their pursuit of Cacciato, noting the different kinds of transportation they used.

Invisible Man, by Ralph Ellison.
New York: Vintage, 1947. 568p. (1)

The "invisibility" in this novel has many interpretations, not the least of which is how people can become invisible to themselves when they allow their lives to be directed by the unexamined will of others—both people and faceless institutions. The saga is told in first person. The reader lives with the nameless narrator through one disillusionment after another: trying to fit in at a stag party; being caught in a college president's scheme to keep the support of a powerful trustee; expulsion from college. There is a series of struggles in New York City: seeking employment; becoming involved with *The Brotherhood*; and a prolonged riot in Harlem. Only with his life collapsing about him does the narrator rediscover himself apart from the puppet roles he has played.

Comment

The novel speaks at some level to everyone, since at one time or another, everyone experiences being a nonperson. The struggle of blacks a decade before the Civil Rights movement is used to exhort all to follow the wisdom of the author's former slave grandfather, "to keep up the good fight" to allow people to become fulfilled and hence the nation to live out its possibilities. The reader also gets inside views of sharecropping, life at an all-black college, hazardous working conditions, and life in substandard housing.

Suggestions for Reports or Activities

1. How can a person become invisible to others? to him or herself? Based on the examples in the book, or drawing from your own experience, write a short paper on this topic.

2. To what extent are Bledsoe, Norton, and Brother Jack, as described in the novel, also depersonalized in their roles?

3. How did blacks returning from World War II military service feel they were being received? Research this in editorials in a black newspaper or *The Crisis* magazine.

4. What kind of black and white relationships does the author suggest would be appropriate for the post-World War II American society?

Journey Home, by Yoshiko Uchida.
New York: Atheneum, 1978. 131p. (3)

At last Yuki Sakane and her parents are on the outside. They have been released from the concentration camp in Utah and are living in an apartment in Salt Lake City. When will they be able to go home, to California, to their own house? After a time they learn that Reverend Wada at a Japanese church in Berkeley has set up a hostel and will sponsor them. But troubles tarnish their new happiness. Jobs for Japanese-Americans are hard to find, vandals ransack the Buddhist temple where many of the evacuees have stored their belongings, and then arsonists attempt to destroy the recently restored Japanese grocery store. Yuki's brother Ken, returning from serving with the American army in France, has a shattered leg and seems strangely withdrawn. Will the Sakanes ever really be at home again?

Comment

In this sequel to *Journey to Topaz*, the author shows the difficulties experienced by Japanese-Americans returning from the camps to pick up the pieces of their lives. Anti-Japanese sentiment took different forms—from personal insults to major criminal incidents. The determination of these people to show themselves loyal Americans and to overcome prejudice while upholding Japanese ideals is strongly portrayed. Readers will experience from a Japanese-American point of view the relief that the war was over combined with the pain of losing loved ones in the bomb attack on Hiroshima.

Suggestions for Reports or Activities

1. What events led to the United States' decision to drop atomic bombs on Hiroshima and Nagasaki? Would you agree that this was the best decision at the time?

2. Uncle Oka does not feel friendly toward Yuki's white friends. Why?

3. One of the important values in Japanese culture is respect for the elderly. Write a short paper on how this value is expressed in the story.

Journey to Topaz, by Yoshiko Uchida.
New York: Scribner, 1971. 149p. (3)

Life changes suddenly for Yuki Sakane and her family on December 7, 1941. After the bombing of Pearl Harbor, all Japanese-Americans living on the West Coast are the objects of suspicion. Because Yuki's father works for a large Japanese business firm, he is immediately taken into custody by the FBI. Yuki's brother Ken leaves the university. Then comes the official order: pack two suitcases and prepare to be evacuated. Mr. Sakane has been sent with other prominent businessmen to a camp in Montana. Yuki with her mother and Ken are finally sent to Topaz, Utah. Anxious to prove their loyalty to the United States, the Sakanes and other internees make the best of an unfortunate and painful situation.

Comment

The fact that during World War II there were actual concentration camps in the United States is little known by young people. This book allows readers to experience the incredulity and fear, the disruption and unhappiness endured by thousands of innocent people in a time of national alarm. The story points up the resourcefulness of the internees, who managed to hold together their lives in spite of difficult living arrangements and material deprivation.

Suggestions for Reports or Activities

1. Read President Roosevelt's order for the evacuation of the Japanese-Americans. What was the reaction in leading newspapers? Compare editorials in a Los Angeles or San Francisco newspaper with commentaries from one or two newspapers from eastern and midwestern cities. Can you notice any difference in attitude toward the evacuation?

2. Who were the Nisei? Why were Yuki's parents considered "enemy aliens"? What were the restrictions against Japanese becoming citizens of the United States? When were changes made in these restrictions?

3. Since the end of the war, has there been any attempt to repay the Japanese internees for any financial losses they suffered as a result of the evacuation?

4. Describe the home that Yuki's family made for themselves at Topaz.

The Last Mission, by Harry Mazer.
New York: Delacorte, 1979. 182p. (2, 3)

Jack Raab is determined to fight Hitler. When the Army turns down his brother Irv because of his rheumatic heart, fifteen-year-old Jack has his chance. Borrowing Irv's birth certificate, he enlists in the air force. Pretending in a note to his parents that he's gone exploring out west, Jack heads for basic training and soon is a gunner on a B-17 bomber. He makes fast friends with the rest of the crew but never reveals his age. They fly twenty-five missions over Germany, narrowly escape after a crash landing in the English Channel, and then their luck runs out. Jack is a prisoner of the Germans when the war in Europe ends. Hitler is dead. And now, he just wants to go home again.

Comment

Based on the author's own World War II experience, this story is an authentic rendering of the close-knit fellowship aboard a B-17. For young readers it is a look at war from the perspective of a young man who yearns to be in the fray of battle, to be a hero saving the Jews from Hitler. A year later though the boyish idea of war is transformed into a grim and painful reality. The occasional use of so-called vulgar terms adds to the reality of conversation among soldiers.

Suggestions for Reports or Activities

1. Read about the Allied bombing of Germany. What major cities were targets? What important historic buildings were destroyed?

2. Jack's actions caused considerable pain for his family. Do you feel that he was justified or unjustified in running away to join the air force? Why?

3. What do you think happens to Jack after the story ends? How will he get along with young people his own age who simply stayed at home and went to high school?

A Necessary End, by Nathaniel Benchley.
New York: Harper & Row, 1976. 193p. (1, 2)

Ralph, a new navy recruit, has received a diary as a seventeenth birthday gift from his family. Following his English teacher's advice, he begins recording all the details in case it should be published one day. He is assigned to a PC, or submarine chaser, patrolling the Atlantic coastal waters for German submarines. Ralph thinks it's pretty boring duty. But there are some laughs, and he does take part in some amusing escapades. Although letters from home are eagerly awaited, his family sends advice about keeping his feet dry; letters from his best girl become shorter and fewer. Ralph knows that he is becoming a different person because of his new life. Then suddenly his ship is ordered to the Pacific, and here he finds that the war is very real. Two months after Hiroshima, Ralph's ship is escorting occupation troop ships through mine-infested waters. He sends his diary home to his teacher—just in case.

Comment

The poignant depiction of a young man growing and changing under harsh circumstances shows how the war affected young American enlisted men. As the author states, "The men at the lower levels have no sense of global strategy; they have, very simply, the fervent hope they will survive the twin enemies of man: hostile action and boredom." In the background is the progress of World War II: the end of the Atlantic conflict; the intensified action in the Pacific; President Roosevelt's death; and the bombing of Hiroshima and Nagasaki.

Suggestions for Reports or Activities

1. Ralph's ship is patrolling the Atlantic coast for submarines, which he considers a boring assignment. Find out about the threat to the U.S. mainland from German submarines. Write a short paper on the importance of this duty.

2. In the front of the book, the author quotes a passage from Shakespeare. Did you notice it before you read the book? How does this hint make the conclusion inevitable? Write another ending for the story and suggest another title for the book.

3. Research how World War II was fought on the seas. Discuss it in a short paper.

One More Time, by Charles Ferry.
Boston: Houghton Mifflin, 1985. 171p. (2)

The Gene Markham Orchestra is on its last cross-country tour, as Skeets Sinclair, the clarinetist, tells the story. The United States has just been plunged into World War II. Because the bandleader has enlisted, the number-two band in the country will have to break up. The members have grown to depend on each other. This last trip is a time of remembering, of appreciating, and of questioning as they travel by bus and train between one-night stands from college campus to military base to club. The war is beginning to reach into all of their lives. Some band members are finding draft notices in the mail. Gus, the manager, has not heard from his son in the Pacific. What about the combo Skeets hopes to start? And what about Polly, the vocalist? Everyone's in love with her, but Skeets is seriously smitten. What will happen to everyone?

Comment

World War II in some of its aspects and effects on people in America is effectively evoked through the hopes and fears of the band members. In the background are comments about the draft, rationing, new jobs in defense plants, German U-boats off the New Jersey coast, the bombing of Tokyo.

Entertaining the troops was an important role for bands and other entertainers. A racial incident at a hotel in Detroit shows the reality of prejudice in the North in the 1940s. The author has created an historical atmosphere in which the uncertainties caused by the war are mirrored in the concerns of the characters.

Suggestions for Reports or Activities

1. What were the regulations for enlistment in military service during World War II? Why was Skeets 4-F? How did Harry get deferred?

2. The big band was a phenomenon of American life. Write a short paper on the rise of the big band. Or select one of the famous bandleaders (Benny Goodman, Harry James, Count Basie, Glen Miller, for example) and write a short paper on his wartime activities.

Pageant, by Kathryn Lasky.
New York: Four Winds, 1986. 221p. (2, 3)

November for the students at Stuart Hall, a conservative Indianapolis prep school, means rehearsing for the annual Christmas pageant. For Sarah Benjamin, one of only three Kennedy supporters in the school, November 1960 is the beginning of new awareness. The headmistress is furious because Sarah is wearing a "Kennedy for President" button on her shepherd's costume. Why not? wonders Sarah, but she has other questions. Should a Jewish student be a shepherd in a Christmas pageant? Through the next three years, from November to November, her tiny, tidy world begins to change. Her sister Marla goes away to college; her Aunt Hattie, bothersome and pushy, comes for a long stay. A promising date for the Christmas dance ends in disaster. The headmistress rejects her science project. But Sarah is beginning to know herself. Finally, one more pageant is just too much, and on a fateful November day in 1963, Sarah makes a bold move.

Comment

This coming-of-age story is set against the background of the sixties beginning with the election of President Kennedy. The atmosphere of the time is vividly evoked, for example, in the broad vision of optimism in the "New Frontier" and the national mourning at the president's death. The author has also shown, through Sarah's reaction to the little black stableboy lawn statues and to her prom date's comments about blacks, the growing general concern over racial prejudice. Sarah's decision to join the Peace Corps reflects the idealism of college-age youth at that time.

Suggestions for Reports or Activities

1. What was the "New Frontier?" What were the larger goals of the Kennedy administration? What was accomplished?

2. Sarah decides to join the Peace Corps. What is the Peace Corps? What are the requirements to become a volunteer? Write a short paper on the Peace Corps then and now.

3. Why is the title *Pageant* appropriate for this book?

Raspberry One, by Charles Ferry.
Boston: Houghton Mifflin, 1983. 232p. (2, 3)

For so many young men and women during World War II, life was to be lived for the moment because life was precious. Yet they did not know what war really meant. While awaiting their orders to ship out to the Pacific, Nick and Hildy, two young crewmen on a navy bomber, strike up a merry friendship with college sophomores Fran and Diane. By the time their orders come, Franny and Nick are engaged and determined to work out an interfaith marriage when the war is over. The story shifts then to the Pacific, to the frightening experience of the Japanese kamikaze offensive and the struggle to control Iwo Jima. Nick and Hildy's plane, *Raspberry One*, is shot down and their loved senior officer killed. Although Nick and Hildy are both seriously wounded (Nick loses a hand, and Hildy probably will never have full use of one leg), they do return, inevitably wise beyond their years, and ready to take adult responsibility for their lives.

Comment

Based partly on the author's own experience, *Raspberry One* shows how the war created intense friendships, wrecked lives, and forced young people to grow. The pain and terror, excitement and carnage aboard an aircraft carrier in the midst of bombing attacks are described graphically. In addition to experiencing feelings of young men in wartime, such as deep devotion to friend and officer, readers will learn of the actual operation of a navy bomber and of the magnitude of the Pacific operation. The fate of European Jews and the bombing of Hiroshima and Nagasaki are also discussed.

Suggestions for Reports or Activities

1. Is the author correct in his description of the training of the crew for *Raspberry One*? Research the preparation of bomber crews during World War II.

2. Iwo Jima is discussed in considerable detail. Look up Iwo Jima in an encyclopedia or other source. Where is it located? What was its importance to the Allied forces? Can you locate a copy of the famous photograph of the flag-raising on Iwo Jima?

3. From what you have been studying about World War II, and from the experiences of the war in the Pacific described in this book, do you feel that the United States was justified in dropping atom bombs on Hiroshima and Nagasaki? Discuss.

Rumors of Peace, by Ella Leffland.
New York: Harper, 1979. 389p. (1, 2)

Suse, living in the small oil-refining town of Mendoza, California, and hoping to be a trapeze artist, is only eleven when the Japanese bomb Pearl Harbor. But she takes on the war as her own special project. In her insatiable curiosity she wants desperately to understand what is happening and why. At first she has extreme opinions—all Japanese are spies; all Germans are Nazis. She is deeply affected by movie newsreels and photographs of casualties. What do they mean? Always questioning, she turns to her friend Helen Maria, a "genius" who is graduating from Berkeley at fifteen, hoping for answers. Are there any? As the war progresses and as she watches the headlines, Suse grows up. She is also becoming aware of herself, of her capabilities, of her awakening sexuality. At the end of the novel and the end of the war, she senses that there are no satisfactory answers, but she knows that the sun shines anyway.

Comment

This story gives the reader a look at World War II from the viewpoint of a curious and intelligent young person. Suse's opinions and concerns bubble forth as she experiences blackouts, air raid drill alerts, and rationing, and becomes aware of the Japanese removal. Headlines from the war front mark the passage of time. The book records the feelings of exhilaration at the end of the war in Europe, and the tentative jubilation when the atomic bomb brings Japan to its knees.

Suggestions for Reports or Activities

1. Suse lived on the West Coast, where people were afraid of a possible Japanese attack. Check in some California newspapers of December 1941 and early 1942. Write a short paper on attitudes reflected in letters to the editor.

2. All through the book Suse is trying to know and understand more about the war. She seems to be looking for a simple explanation. Do you think that she has learned anything as a result of her quest? In a short paper, indicate what you think Suse has been able to find out.

3. If you could change the ending of the book, how would you do it? You may change the last chapter, or create an additional concluding chapter. What will Suse do now?

Summer of My German Soldier, by Bette Greene.
New York: Dial, 1973. 230p. (3)

Excitement comes to the sleepy town of Jenkinsville, Arkansas, one summer when a camp is set up there for German prisoners of war. For Patty Bergen it means a small break in the monotony and unhappiness of her life. Bright and outspoken, she seems able only to antagonize her unfeeling parents, proprietors of a small department store. Patty's only real friend is the black housekeeper, until the day she hides an escaped German prisoner in the room over her family garage. Anton appreciates Patty and treats her as "a person of value." He has to move on, and Patty is unable to keep secret the ring he has given her, although she invents a story about its origin. When it is finally revealed that Patty, whose family is Jewish, has sheltered a Nazi soldier, the town is in an uproar and Patty is sent to a reform school. But she knows that she cannot be kept down forever.

Comment

The presence of German prisoners on the outskirts of the town added fuel to the already hot anti-German sentiments. Greene shows how suspicion builds in tense times. The latent anti-Semitism of the townspeople is also revealed. Anton, the German prisoner, is depicted as far more compassionate and intelligent than most of the people of Jenkinsville.

Suggestions for Reports or Activities

1. Stereotyping, using the same label to apply to everyone in a group, is especially likely to occur in times of tension, such as during a war. Discuss some of the stereotypes that Americans have used at different periods of this century.

2. Check some newspaper accounts of hysteria in the United States over enemy nationals within U.S. borders. From the perspective of today, was this attitude justified? Discuss.

3. If you have not read the sequel of this book, how would you continue Patty's story? How does this memorable summer affect her life?

To Stand against the Wind, by Ann Nolan Clark.
New York: Viking, 1978. 136p. (3)

Eleven-year-old Em is now in America, with his grandmother and Old Uncle, and his older sister, Chi-Bah. It has been one year since the dreadful day that changed forever a family and their traditional way of life. Now, on the Day of the Ancestors, it is Em's task, as head of the family, to record memories of Vietnam and of what happened to loved ones. It is hard, but he must try. So he remembers and tries to write about the hamlet where his family lived for generations; about his parents and how the war gradually was everywhere around them; and about his beloved water buffalo; and about Sam, the American reporter, who was his dear friend. He recalls it all, but on the paper he can put only an old proverb learned from his father: "It takes a strong man to stand against the wind."

Comment

This story introduces readers to Vietnam before and during the war. It shows the Vietnamese as a gentle, thoughtful, disciplined people with a deep respect for their ancient traditions. Em's story emphasizes the Vietnamese belief in the importance of the family, respect for elders, knowing one's role, acceptance of fate. The horror of the killing of innocent villagers, the bewilderment and frustration of the American soldiers, and the dislocation of the war victims are vividly portrayed through Em's stories.

Suggestions for Reports or Activities

1. Some Vietnamese customs are described. Based on what you have learned from the book, write a short paper on the celebration of Tet or on the traditional arrangements for a wedding.

2. What was the Tet Offensive in the Vietnam War?

3. What is the meaning of the title, taken from a Vietnamese proverb?

4. If possible, talk to someone who came to the United States as a result of the war. Ask if he or she would be willing to share some experiences.

A Woman of Independent Means, by Elizabeth Forsythe Hailey. New York: Viking, 1978. 256p. (1)

This story is told entirely in the form of letters from Elizabeth Alcott Steed Garner, known as Bess, to members of her family, to friends, and to business associates. The first letter is to her fourth-grade sweetheart, later her first husband, and the last is to welcome her new great-grandchild. In between are covered nearly seventy years of history, political as well as personal. Through her letters the reader comes to know Bess and also to experience the major events of the period through their effect on her life and thinking.

Comment

Bess's perspective, as "a woman of independent means," should not be generalized too widely. Yet many of the events that affected her life touched the lives of Americans from other parts of the country and other social and economic levels as well. Wars were important, of course, but so were gradual changes in race relations, women's rights, and even American concepts of justice and fair play. Bess's development from a woman not only independent but unbearably domineering surely reflects in part the changing times in which she lived.

Suggestions for Reports or Activities

1. Bess, her daughter Eleanor, and her granddaughter Betsy all show their independence but in different ways. Name some of these ways and tell how they reflect the changing values of the society of the time.

2. Find the part in the book where Bess writes an angry letter to Eleanor. Write a letter from Eleanor in response to her mother's complaints.

3. Bess mentions once that she cannot sell her house, which is in her name alone, because her husband Sam will not consent. Research the current laws of Texas to see if this situation would prevail today.

AUTHOR-TITLE INDEX

Prepared by Julie M. Mueller

Across Five Aprils, 33
After the Dancing Days, 85
Alan and Naomi, 115
Aldrich, Bess S. *A Lantern in Her Hand,* 69
All the King's Men, 101
Allen, Hervey. *The Forest and the Fort,* 4
Anderson, Joan. *1787,* 26
Andersonville, 34
Appointment in Samarra, 102
April Harvest, 86
April Morning, 13
Arnold, Elliott. *The Camp Grant Massacre,* 61
Arnow, Harriette. *The Dollmaker,* 117
Arrest Sitting Bull, 57
Arundel, 14
The Autobiography of Miss Jane Pittman, 34
Avi. *The Fighting Ground,* 17

Beatty, Patricia. *Turn Homeward Hannalee,* 51; *Wait for Me, Watch for Me, Eula Bee,* 82
Benchley, Nathaniel. *A Necessary End,* 124; *Only Earth and Sky Last Forever,* 74
Berger, Thomas. *Little Big Man,* 71
Bess, Clayton. *Tracks,* 111
Beyond the Divide, 58
The Big Sky, 58
The Bloody Country, 14
Blos, Joan. *Brothers of the Heart,* 60; *A Gathering of Days,* 40
Bohner, Charles. *Bold Journey,* 59
Bold Journey, 59
Boyd, James. *Drums,* 16
Bradley, David. *The Chaneysville Incident,* 37
Brady, 35
Branson, Karen. *Streets of Gold,* 98
The Bridges at Toko-ri, 116

Bring Home the Ghost, 36
Brothers of the Heart, 60
Brown, Dee. *Creek Mary's Blood,* 64; *Killdeer Mountain,* 69
Brown, Rita Mae. *High Hearts,* 42
Budd, Lillian. *April Harvest,* 86
Burr, 15

Cahan, Abraham. *The Rise of David Levinsky,* 95
Calico Bush, 1
Calico Captive, 2
Calvert, Patricia. *The Snowbird,* 80
The Camp Grant Massacre, 61
Caribou, 116
Cather, Willa. *My Antonia,* 73
Cavanna, Betty. *Ruffles and Drums,* 24
The Chaneysville Incident, 37
Cheatham, K. Follis. *Bring Home the Ghost,* 36
Cimarron, 62
Circle of Fire, 102
Clapp, Patricia. *Constance,* 2; *I'm Deborah Sampson,* 19; *The Tamarack Tree,* 48; *Witches' Children,* 11
Clark, Ann Nolan. *To Stand against the Wind,* 129
Clark, Walter van Tilburg. *The Ox-Bow Incident,* 76
Clauser, Suzanne. *A Girl Named Sooner,* 104
Collier, Christopher. *The Bloody Country,* 14; *Jump Ship to Freedom,* 21; *My Brother Sam Is Dead,* 22; *War Comes to Willie Freeman,* 29; *The Winter Hero,* 30; *Who Is Carrie?* 29
Collier, James Lincoln. *The Bloody Country,* 14; *Jump Ship to Freedom,* 21; *My Brother Sam Is Dead,* 22; *War Comes to Willie Freeman,* 29; *The Winter Hero,* 30; *Who Is Carrie?* 29

133

Conrad, Pam. *Prairie Songs*, 77
Constance, 2
A Country of Strangers, 3
The Court-Martial of George Armstrong Custer, 62
Cowslip, 38
Craven, Margaret. *Walk Gently This Good Earth*, 112
Crazy Weather, 63
Creek Mary's Blood, 64
Cummings, Betty Sue. *Hew against the Grain*, 42; *Now Ameriky*, 92

The Dark Didn't Catch Me, 103
Davis, Paxton. *Three Days*, 51
Doctorow, E. L. *Ragtime*, 94
The Dollmaker, 117
Dos Passos, John. *Manhattan Transfer*, 108
Dragonwings, 87
Dreiser, Theodore. *Sister Carrie*, 96
Drums, 16
Dunbar, Paul Laurence. *The Sport of the Gods*, 97

Elkhorn Tavern, 38
Ellison, Ralph. *Invisible Man*, 121

Fallen Angels, 118
Farber, Norma. *Mercy Short*, 6
Fast, Howard. *April Morning*, 13; *Freedom Road*, 39; *The Hessian*, 18
Ferber, Edna. *Cimarron*, 62
Ferry, Charles. *One More Time*, 125; *Raspberry One*, 127
Field, Rachel. *Calico Bush*, 1
The Fighting Ground, 17
Fitzgerald, F. Scott. *The Great Gatsby*, 105
Fletcher, Inglis. *Lusty Wind for Carolina*, 6
Forbes, Esther. *Johnny Tremain*, 21
Foreman, James D. *Freedom's Blood*, 120
The Forest and the Fort, 4
Fox, Paula. *The Slave Dancer*, 46
Fragments, 119
Franchere, Ruth. *Hannah Herself*, 66
Freedom Road, 39
Freedom's Blood, 120
Freelon Starbird, 17
Fritz, Jean. *Brady*, 35
Fuller, Jack. *Fragments*, 119

Gaines, Ernest J. *The Autobiography of Miss Jane Pittman*, 34
A Gathering of Days, 40
Gently Touch the Milkweed, 65
Geras, Adele. *Voyage*, 99
Giants in the Earth, 65
A Girl Named Sooner, 104
Going after Cacciato, 120
Gone with the Wind, 41
The Grapes of Wrath, 104
The Great Gatsby, 105
Greene, Bette. *Summer of My German Soldier*, 128
Guthrie, A. B. *The Big Sky*, 58; *The Way West*, 83

Hailey, Elizabeth Forsythe. *A Woman of Independent Means*, 130
Haley, Alex. *Roots*, 45
Hall, Lynn. *Gently Touch the Milkweed*, 65
Hannah Herself, 66
Hansen, Joyce. *Which Way Freedom?* 54
Haynes, Betsy. *Cowslip*, 38
Heidish, Marcy. *A Woman Called Moses*, 55
The Hessian, 18
Hew against the Grain, 42
High Hearts, 42
Hooks, William H. *Circle of Fire*, 102
Hotchner, A. E. *King of the Hill*, 106
The House of Mirth, 87
Hunt, Irene. *Across Five Aprils*, 33; *No Promises in the Wind*, 109
Hurmence, Belinda. *Tancy*, 49

I'm Deborah Sampson, 19
In the Shadow of the Wind, 67
Invisible Man, 121

John Treegate's Musket, 20
Johnny Tremain, 21
Jones, Douglas C. *Arrest Sitting Bull*, 57; *The Court-Martial of George Armstrong Custer*, 62; *Elkhorn Tavern*, 38; *Season of Yellow Leaf*, 77
Journey Home, 122
Journey to Topaz, 123
Jubilee, 43
Jump Ship to Freedom, 21
The Jungle, 88

Kantor, MacKinlay. *Andersonville*, 34
The Keeping-Room, 68
Keith, Harold. *Rifles for Watie*, 44
Killdeer Mountain, 69
King of the Hill, 106

LaFarge, Oliver. *Laughing Boy*, 70
Lane, Rose Wilder. *Young Pioneers*, 84
A Lantern in Her Hand, 69
Lasky, Kathryn. *Beyond the Divide*, 58;
    Pageant, 126
The Last Mission, 123
The Late George Apley, 89
Laughing Boy, 70
Lee, Mildred. *The Rock and the Willow*, 110
Leffland, Ella. *Rumors of Peace*, 128
Lester, Julius. *This Strange New Feeling*, 50
Let the Circle Be Unbroken, 107
Let the Hurricane Roar, 84
Levin, Betty. *The Keeping-Room*, 68
Levitin, Sonia. *The No-Return Trail*, 73;
    Roanoke, 7
Levoy, Myron. *Alan and Naomi*, 115
Lewis, Sinclair. *Main Street*, 91
The Light in the Forest, 5
Little Big Man, 71
Lusty Wind for Carolina, 6

The Magnificent Ambersons, 90
Magnuson, James. *Orphan Train*, 75
Main Street, 91
Manhattan Transfer, 108
Marquand, John P. *The Late George Apley*,
    89
The Massacre at Fall Creek, 72
Mays, Lucinda. *The Other Shore*, 93
Mazer, Harry. *The Last Mission*, 123
McNichols, Charles. *Crazy Weather*, 63
Mercy Short, 6
Michener, James A. *The Bridges of Toko-ri*,
    116
Mitchell, Margaret. *Gone with the Wind*, 41
My Antonia, 73
My Brother Sam Is Dead, 22
Myers, Walter Dean. *Fallen Angels*, 118

Native Son, 108
A Necessary End, 124
No Promises in the Wind, 109
The No-Return Trail, 73

Norris, Frank. *The Pit: A Story of Chicago*,
    93
Now Ameriky, 92

O'Brien, Tim. *Going after Cacciato*, 120
O'Dell, Scott. *Sarah Bishop*, 25; *Sing Down
    the Moon*, 79; *Streams to the River, River
    to the Sea*, 81; *The 290*, 52
O'Hara, John. *Appointment in Samarra*, 102
Oliver Wiswell, 23
One More Time, 125
Only Earth and Sky Last Forever, 74
Orphan Train, 75
The Other Shore, 93
The Ox-Bow Incident, 76

Page, Elizabeth. *The Tree of Liberty*, 28
Pageant, 126
Perez, N. A. *The Slopes of War*, 47
Petrie, Dorothea G. *Orphan Train*, 75
Petry, Ann. *Tituba of Salem Village*, 10
The Pit: A Story of Chicago, 93
Prairie Songs, 77

Rabble in Arms, 24
Ragtime, 94
Raspberry One, 127
Richter, Conrad. *A Country of Strangers*, 3;
    The Light in the Forest, 5
Rifles for Watie, 44
Rinaldi, Ann. *Time Enough for Drums*, 27
The Rise of David Levinsky, 95
Roanoke, 7
Roberts, Kenneth. *Arundel*, 14; *Oliver
    Wiswell*, 23; *Rabble in Arms*, 24
The Rock and the Willow, 110
Roll of Thunder, Hear My Cry, 111
Rolvaag, Ole. *Giants in the Earth*, 65
Roots, 45
Rostkowski, Margaret I. *After the Dancing
    Days*, 85
Ruffles and Drums, 24
Rumors of Peace, 128

The Sacred Moon Tree, 46
Sarah Bishop, 25
Schaefer, Jack. *Shane*, 78
Season of Yellow Leaf, 77
1787, 26
Shane, 78

Shore, Laura Jan. *The Sacred Moon Tree*, 46
The Sign of the Beaver, 8
Sinclair, Upton. *The Jungle*, 88
Sing Down the Moon, 79
Sister Carrie, 96
Skurzynski, Gloria. *The Tempering*, 98
The Slave Dancer, 46
The Slopes of War, 47
Smith, Claude Clayton. *The Stratford Devil*, 9
Snow, Richard E. *Freelon Starbird*, 17
The Snowbird, 80
The Sodbuster Venture, 80
Speare, Elizabeth George. *Calico Captive*, 2; *The Sign of the Beaver*, 8; *The Witch of Blackbird Pond*, 10
The Sport of the Gods, 97
Steinbeck, John. *The Grapes of Wrath*, 104
The Stratford Devil, 9
Streams to the River, River to the Sea, 81
Streets of Gold, 98
Summer of My German Soldier, 128

Talbot, Charlene Joy. *The Sodbuster Venture*, 80
The Tamarack Tree, 48
Tancy, 49
Tarkington, Booth. *The Magnificent Ambersons*, 90
Taylor, Mildred, D. *Let the Circle Be Unbroken*, 107; *Roll of Thunder, Hear My Cry*, 111
The Tempering, 98
This Strange New Feeling, 50
Thrasher, Crystal. *The Dark Didn't Catch Me*, 103
Three Days, 51
Time Enough for Drums, 27
Tituba of Salem Village, 10

To Stand against the Wind, 129
Tracks, 111
The Tree of Liberty, 28
Turn Homeward, Hannalee, 51
The 290, 52

Uchida, Yoshiko. *Journey Home*, 122; *Journey to Topaz*, 123
Unto This Hour, 53

Vidal, Gore. *Burr*, 15
Voyage, 99

Wait for Me, Watch for Me, Eula Bee, 82
Walk Gently This Good Earth, 112
Walker, Margaret. *Jubilee*, 43
Wallin, Luke. *In the Shadow of the Wind*, 67
War Comes to Willie Freeman, 29
Warren, Robert Penn. *All the King's Men*, 101
The Way West, 83
West, Jessamyn. *The Massacre at Fall Creek*, 72
Wharton, Edith. *The House of Mirth*, 87
Which Way Freedom? 54
Who Is Carrie? 29
Wibberley, Leonard. *John Treegate's Musket*, 20
Wicker, Tom. *Unto This Hour*, 53
The Winter Hero, 30
The Witch of Blackbird Pond, 10
Witches' Children, 11
Wolitzer, Meg. *Caribou*, 116
A Woman Called Moses, 55
A Woman of Independent Means, 130
Wright, Richard. *Native Son*, 108

Yep, Laurence. *Dragonwings*, 87
Young Pioneers, 84

Elizabeth F. Howard is associate professor in the department of library science at West Virginia University, where she teaches courses in children's and young adult literature. As an active member of ALA, Howard has served on numerous committees, including the Caldecott Award Committee, the ALA-Children's Book Council Liaison Committee, and the Teachers of Children's Literature Discussion Group.